MAJORING IN
THE REST OF
YOUR LIFE

MAJORING IN THE REST OF YOUR LIFE

Career Secrets for College Students

CAROL CARTER

THE NOONDAY PRESS
Farrar, Straus and Giroux
New York

Published in Canada by HarperCollins*CanadaLtd*

Printed in the United States of America

Designed by Nancy Sugihara

First edition, 1990

Seventh printing, 1994

Library of Congress Cataloging-in-Publication Data
Carter, Carol.
    Majoring in the rest of your life : career secrets for college
students / Carol Carter.—1st ed.
        p.   cm.
    1. Vocational guidance—United States.   2. College students—
Employment—United States.   I. Title.
HF5382.5.U5C37   1990   650.14—dc20   89-71526   CIP

"The World of Work: A Sampler" reprinted from the 1987 *What Color Is Your Parachute?* by Richard Nelson Bolles. Copyright © 1987 by Richard Nelson Bolles. Reprinted with permission from Ten Speed Press, P.O. Box 7123, Berkeley, CA 94707.

Excerpt from *Megatrends: Ten New Directions Transforming Our Lives* by John Naisbitt, copyright © 1982 by John Naisbitt, reprinted by permission of Warner Books.

Excerpt from *Working* by Studs Terkel, copyright © 1972, 1974 by Studs Terkel, reprinted by permission of Pantheon Books, a division of Random House, Inc.

Excerpt from *The Right Job* by Robert O. Snelling, Sr., copyright © 1987 by Robert O. Snelling, Sr., reprinted by permission of Penguin Books.

Excerpt from *The Simon & Schuster Handbook for Writers* by Lynn Troyka, copyright © 1987 by Lynn Troyka, reprinted by permission of Prentice Hall.

Excerpt from *The Struggle That Must Be* by Harry Edwards, copyright © 1980 by Harry Edwards, reprinted by permission of Macmillan Publishing Company.

Excerpt from *What They Don't Teach You at Harvard Business School* by Mark McCormack, copyright © 1986 by Mark McCormack, reprinted by permission of Bantam Books.

Excerpt from "Taking the Hype Out of Leadership" (*Fortune*, March 28, 1989) by Andrew S. Grove, reprinted by permission of Andrew S. Grove.

Excerpt from *How to Win Friends and Influence People* by Dale Carnegie and Dorothy Carnegie, copyright © 1936, 1964 by Donna Dale Carnegie and Dorothy Carnegie, reprinted by permission of Simon & Schuster, Inc.

Excerpt from *The Art of the Deal* by Donald Trump, copyright © 1987 by Donald Trump, reprinted by permission of Random House, Inc.

Excerpt from *Thriving on Chaos* by Tom Peters, copyright © 1988 by Tom Peters, reprinted by permission of Harper & Row Publishers, Inc.

Excerpt from *Culture and Value* by Ludwig Wittgenstein, copyright © 1984, reprinted by permission of the University of Chicago Press.

Excerpt from *Getting Work Experience* by Betsy Bauer, copyright © 1985 by Betsy Bauer, reprinted by permission of Dell Publishing Company.

Excerpt from speech by Sandra Day O'Connor, reprinted by permission of Sandra Day O'Connor.

Excerpt from *Ogilvy on Advertising* by David Ogilvy, copyright © 1983 by David Ogilvy, reprinted by permission of Crown Publishers Inc.

Excerpt from *Zen and the Art of Motorcycle Maintenance* by Robert M. Pirsig, copyright © 1974 by Robert M. Pirsig, reprinted by permission of William Morrow & Company.

Excerpt from *Iacocca* by Lee Iacocca, copyright © 1986 by Lee Iacocca, reprinted by permission of Bantam Books.

ACKNOWLEDGMENTS

There are many people woven into the pages of this book whose names do not appear but whose ideas shaped the final manuscript. Some of those people are my dearest friends. Brenda White, John Isley, Madeline Kiser and my brother Scott believed in this book when it was a pipe dream. Throughout the writing process and through moments of self-doubt and inspirational lows, they cheered me on and asked me to be patient.

Numerous people gave me their editorial input—their names are listed at the end of this acknowledgment and their occupations range from freelance writer to schoolteacher to high school senior. One very special influence came from a sophomore at Columbia University, Jeannine Deloche, who spent countless hours interviewing students, rewriting portions of chapters and making suggestions on better ways to explain concepts. Her sound judgment and her ability to disagree with my preconceptions created the best synthesis of ideas.

Paul Bartick, who joined the project in the last three months, kept me going through the final rewrites. His enthusiasm and his ability to make the tedious enjoyable are much appreciated qualities.

Dick Bolles, author of *What Color Is Your Parachute?*, remains my life hero. I only hope that this book can accomplish half as much good as his book has for job seekers.

At Farrar, Straus and Giroux, my editor, Elisabeth Dyssegaard, was terrific. She was enthusiastic about the project from the first time we met and she sent me back to the drawing board a number of times to get the book just right. Although I know she has many other authors, she made me feel as if I were her only one.

My friends—Leigh, Susan, Cynthia, Julie, Anne and Priscilla—showed tremendous support all of those weekends when I was writing and unavailable to play. They also dragged me out when they felt I was spending too much time at the computer.

I would like to thank the people I work with at Prentice Hall, especially my colleagues in the marketing department, and Ed Stanford, who has given me the opportunity to learn, grow, and contribute to the company.

Finally, I want to thank my family. David's editorial eye made me strive to write shorter, tighter sentences; Scott's humor—from baseball analogies to H. L. Mencken references—spiced up the tone of the book as well as my approach to it; Craig's background as a journalist at *Fortune* prompted him to suggest that I interview people from different industries to get their perspectives on the career search. Kent helped me fight against monomania, a disease he thought I had six months before the book was finished!

I owe my deepest appreciation to my parents. They have always counterbalanced the pragmatism of my brothers; they taught me that no dream is too outrageous, no goal out of reach.

My gratitude to the people who read this manuscript (some more than once) and gave me their suggestions on how it could be improved: Paul Alloca, Ron Avendinko, Ed Azary, Chris Barnett, Paul Bartick, Kim Caldwell-Meeks, Patti Carr, Jeff Carver, Terry Condon, Steve Dale, Jeannine Deloche, Merlene Dirielyan, Martin D'Luzansky, Cynthia Fox, Lisa Fumia, Rachel Fumia, John Isley, Linda Jacobs, Gary June, Joanne Karpe, David Lambert, Diane Lasky, Priscilla McGeehon, Karen McMillan, Darren Palmet, Vince Perez, Jon Perkins, Joyce Perkins, Jennifer Plane, Elizabeth Prince, Adrian Ramirez, Anne Riddick, Jen Salzar, Elizabeth Scarpelli, Charles Sherry, Brian Sahd, Leigh Talmage, Bud and Bonnie Therien and Cyrus Vesser.

For my parents, John and Mary, and my brothers, David, Scott, Craig and Kent, who have always provided the balance between being demanding and being supportive

CONTENTS

Appendices

MAJORING IN
THE REST OF
YOUR LIFE

INTRODUCTION

Dear Freshman

Majoring in the Rest of Your Life can help you choose a career and give you specific suggestions to get you from your freshman to your senior year and on to the job of your dreams. It makes no difference whether you've already selected a career. Just keep your mind open. All that's necessary, really, is for you to commit yourself to getting a good education, setting career goals and then working to reach them.

Genius Need Not Apply

This book probably can't help the aspiring ballerina or brain surgeon. Their success will depend more on their natural abilities than on what it might teach them. Likewise, it will prove worthless to the student content with an entry-level position. But between genius and the unaspiring are the vast majority of students—people like you and me.

For Example?

Mark Garrety graduated from the University of Washington with a history degree and a 3.9 grade average. Four months later he still hadn't found a job.

Sharon Heider partied through four years at the University of Georgia. She was a marketing major with mediocre grades. Everybody loved her. Now she's a bank teller. People still love her. But she's unhappy and thinks a degree should be bankable for more than $12,000 a year.

José Rodríguez is a senior at Northwestern. He's made good grades, worked part-time in the library and served as campus coordinator for the United Way. What will he do after graduation? Jose has no clue. Law school, maybe.

Then there's you. You're browsing through these pages wondering why you should read this book. Will it really help you get a job once you're out of school?

Yes. It will help you analyze your interests and decide what you do and don't like in and out of school, and it will give you advice on how to get from your first freshman class to your first job.

By reading this book and taking action, you'll be one giant step closer to the job you want. The job that stimulates you, motivates you, challenges you, inspires the best in you. The job that is invigorating as well as rewarding.

But that's what everybody wants, you say. True, but it's not what everybody gets. Why?

Because most of us are ill-prepared in two areas: self-awareness and planning. Put simply, you must first know what you want and then devise a strategy that will enable you to get it. These skills aren't typically taught in college. They are common-sense secrets that one learns readily on the job. But they *can* be learned in school. In fact, if you learn them early, you'll have an enormous advantage once you're out working.

Second, few people in college bother to get good advice. They fail to realize that there are all kinds of people whose perspective on college, jobs and life can greatly benefit them. This book gives you lots of examples of how people in college and at work continue their education, build their skills and enjoy themselves. You'll see that there are many different methods to achieve success. And you'll learn how to develop relationships with people: how to get help from them and how to give help yourself.

Third, this book will show you not only how to recognize opportunity but how to ACT on it. Seizing the moment is as important as thinking things through. You'll learn how to make your pipe dreams real.

Most important, you will learn to recognize your own unique potential. This is not a way of looking at the world that puts you at the top by placing everybody else at the bottom. On the contrary. It is a way to understand that everyone can succeed.

You will take this knowledge and experience and put it to work for you. You will learn to overcome the fears and doubts which limit your ability to go after what you want. Bottom line: you will learn to tap your own internal resources and talents.

So remember, the only person you have to compete with is you. You know the dialogue between your ego and alter ego: one says "Go for it" while the other screams "No way, I'm scared." You'll learn to bring these two sides into line so that YOU can really work for YOU.

Okay, you say. I'm ready. But maybe I don't know what I want to do.

No problem. This book will help you define your skills and interests so you can choose a career. Maybe you screwed up in high school. Okay, college is a clean slate. Maybe academics aren't your strong suit. Well, you can strengthen your weak suit and finesse your strong ones into a winning hand. (The classroom isn't the only proving ground.) Maybe you've never held a job or joined a club. All right, you can start now.

You'll use this book throughout your college career. So the earlier you read it, the better. If you're a freshman, great. If you're a senior, that's fine too. It will teach you valuable business lessons which will help you in your first job.

How can *Majoring in the Rest of Your Life* best serve you? Read it from cover to cover the summer before or during your freshman year. That will give you a broad overview. As you go from one year to the next, you can refer to the book as necessary. You'll have little need for the information on landing a job your freshman year, but it is useful to know at the outset what kinds of things you'll have to prepare for down the road. After reading this book once, keep it on your reference shelf next to your dictionary and textbooks.

Life Skills

Each chapter in *Majoring in the Rest of Your Life* will help you both in college and out. The "tools" for success are categorized below, but you will learn their true meaning in the context of real-life situations in school and, later, at work. For now, just take note of each skill.

If you master these skills in college, chances are you will have a greater chance of succeeding scholastically. Think of the categories below as life skills. Though few people are adept at all of them, becoming good at some of them is a significant accomplishment. Decide which skills you have. Then think about the ones you want to work on and develop over the next few years.

1. *Write Your Own Success Story*

Planning/Organizing The ability to define specific points of action for yourself and others which will allow you to set priorities and get a job—or goal—completed successfully.

2. *Discover Who You Are*

Problem Solving/Analytical Skills The ability to analyze and identify problems, determine their causes and make suggestions for resolving them. The ability to take positive action.

3. *Futures and Options*

Creativity/Innovativeness The ability to let your mind wander; to discern larger patterns and relationships, to see the overall as well as the detail-filled picture.

4. *Take the Plunge*

Drive/Energy The sheer energy to get the most out of your courses and your professors while balancing your work and activities. The ability to be productive over long hours; to go above and beyond what's required.

5. *Stand Up and Be Counted*

Teamwork The ability to work with others toward a common goal; to be supportive of their ideas and to focus on the goals of the group.

People Management The ability to work with a group by helping each member to set and define personal and group goals; to delegate responsibility and to give constant credit to those who participate.

Leadership The ability to influence others in a positive, motivating way; to command attention and respect.

6. *The Real World*

Common-Sense Smarts The ability to know how things work in the "real world"; to know instinctively what to do in different kinds of situations.

7. *Intern We Trust*

Independence/Tenacity The ability to be unconventional; to take a stand on something which you firmly believe in, but which may be unpopular with a larger group.

8. *Windows on the World* — **Personal Adaptability** The ability to adjust quickly to any situation, group of people or environment; to use past experiences to measure new ones and respond nondefensively to criticism.

9. *Networking* — **Communication** The ability to articulate your thoughts well both on paper and orally; to speak effectively one on one as well as in groups.

10. *Paperwork* — **Marketing Yourself** The ability to make a clear and convincing presentation to those whom you want to persuade.

11. *Your Third Degree* — **Interpersonal Skills** The ability to talk openly and freely with others; to put them at ease with you and to exude confidence and enthusiasm.

12. *You're Hired!* — **Stress Tolerance** The ability to cope in stressful or discouraging situations; to keep things in perspective.

13. *Outlooks and Insights* — **Results/Goal-Oriented** The ability to set measurable and attainable goals; to be motivated by the challenge of achieving them.

At the end of each year, refer to this list. Where have you made progress? Where do you need to improve? What specific goals will you set to help you improve?

· 1 ·

WRITE YOUR OWN SUCCESS STORY
Planning Ahead

I'm a great believer in luck, and I find the harder I work, the more I have of it.
THOMAS JEFFERSON

We have an extraordinary leverage and influence—individually, professionally, and institutionally—if we can only get a clear sense, a clear conception, a clear vision of the road ahead.

JOHN NAISBITT, *Megatrends*

Who am I to talk to high school graduates and college freshmen about planning? As a high school student in Tucson, Arizona, I never planned. I just coasted along letting things happen to me. Sure, I was spontaneous. I spent weeknights talking on the phone and studied only when I felt like it—i.e., seldom. On weekends my friends and I roamed shopping malls and partied in the mountains. The typical irresponsible high school student.

And then BOOM. The ax fell. The ax was not some accident, scandal or divine intervention. It was simply a conversation with my older brother Craig during the first week of my senior year in high school. Our talk changed the course of my life.

At seventeen I was intimidated by my four older brothers. I saw them as bright, motivated and respected achievers—the opposite of me. Whenever one of them asked me about what I was doing or thinking, I'd answer with a one-liner and hope he'd soon leave me alone.

This conversation with Craig was different. He didn't give up after five minutes despite my curt, vague responses.

"Carol, what are you interested in?"

"I dunno."

9

"What do you think about all day?"

"I dunno."

"What do you want to do with your life?"

"I'll just let things happen."

Craig persisted. His voice grew indignant. He criticized me for talking on the phone, for spending too much time at pep rallies and rock concerts, for not studying, for not challenging myself. He pointed out that I hadn't read an unassigned book in three years. He asked if I intended to approach college the way I'd approached high school—as one continuous party. If so, he warned, I'd better start thinking of a career flipping burgers at the local hamburger stand because no respectable employer would ever take me seriously. He asked me if that was what I wanted to do with my life. He cautioned that out of laziness and lack of planning I would limit my options so narrowly that I would never be able to get a real job. I had wasted three years of high school, he said. College was a new start, since employers and graduate schools seldom check as far back as high school for records. So he advised me to quit making excuses, decide what I wanted and plan how to achieve it. My only limitations would be self-imposed.

Craig then left my room—sermon completed. I didn't speak to him before he flew back to New York that afternoon to finish his senior year at Columbia. I hated him for interfering in my life. He made me dissatisfied with myself. I was scared he was right. For the first time, I realized that "typical" was not necessarily what I wanted to be.

The next day, still outraged but determined to do something, I went to the library and checked out six classics: *Pride and Prejudice* by Jane Austen; *The Great Gatsby* by F. Scott Fitzgerald; *A Farewell to Arms* and *For Whom the Bell Tolls* by Ernest Hemingway; *A Portrait of the Artist as a Young Man* by James Joyce; and *Sister Carrie* by Theodore Dreiser. Then I wrote down in a notebook a few goals that I wanted to accomplish. They all seemed boldly unattainable: earn straight A's (previously I had made B's and C's), study every week including one weekend night, keep reading classics on my own. If I couldn't make it in my senior year of high school, why should I waste time and money in college? I'd beat fate to the door and begin my career at the hamburger stand directly.

Three weeks later I got a letter from Craig. He knew how angry I was with him. He told me our conversation wasn't easy for him either but if he hadn't cared, he wouldn't have bothered to say anything. He was right. I needed that sermon. If I didn't come to terms with my problems, I could never have moved from making excuses to making things happen.

I worked hard and got results. The second semester of my senior year I made all A's (except for a B in physics). I finished the six classics and others as well. I started reading newspapers and magazines. I had to move the *Vogue* on my nightstand to make room for *Time, Harper's* and *Fortune*. I found that I could set goals and attain them, and I started to realize that I wasn't so different from my brothers after all.

To my utter astonishment, I discovered that for the first time I enjoyed learning. My world seemed to open up just because I knew more about different kinds of people, ways of thinking and ways of interpreting what I had previously assumed to be black-and-white. (If you are a shy person, joining a club and getting to know—and actually like—a few people whom you originally perceived as unfriendly or uninteresting may astonish you as much as my newfound appreciation for learning astonished me.)

The summer before college, I thought about what I wanted to do with my life, but couldn't decide on a direction. I had no notion of what I wanted to major in. What to do . . . what to do?

I turned to Craig, a phone call away in New York City. He told me not to worry about what I wanted to do in my first year of college. The main priority: learn as much as I could. College, he told me, was my golden opportunity to investigate all kinds of things—biology, psychology, accounting, philosophy. He told me I'd become good at writing and critical thinking techniques—skills that would help me learn any job after graduation. And though I could continue to expand my educational horizons throughout life, college was the best opportunity to expose myself to the greatest minds and movements of our civilization.

Craig also warned me that being a scholar, though important, wouldn't be enough. (He had just graduated from Columbia as a Phi Beta Kappa, but since he hadn't gained any real-world experience in college, it took him several months to find his first job.) To maximize options upon graduation, I would have to do three things:

1. Learn as much as possible from classes, books, professors and other people
2. Participate in extracurricular activities
3. Get REAL-WORLD experience by working part-time and landing summer internships

If I did these three things reasonably well, Craig assured me, I could choose from a number of career opportunities at the end of my senior year. And even if I only did two of the three full-force and one half-speed, I'd be in good shape. The effort in each area, and a modest outcome, was an attainable goal. That way I could balance my college experience and open options for the future.

Craig advised me that I should look ahead and develop a plan of action for each of my four years of college. He told me that foresight—the ability to consider the bigger picture beyond short-term challenges and intermittent goals—is invaluable in most jobs; it distinguishes outstanding people from the rest of the pack.

This book is designed to be for you what Craig was for me—my adviser during college. The following chapters will provide you with guidelines for success by asking you to examine yourself, set goals and believe in your ability to achieve them. It will give you specific examples of how to get things done. It will also introduce you to all kinds of people, all of whom followed their own varying, yet similar paths toward their goals. Most important, you'll learn that everyone—including YOU—has his or her own set of skills, abilities, passions and talents to tap. Finding the career and lifestyle that allows you to cultivate and nurture them is one of the most important success secrets.

So Take Action!

A good way to start is to assess your shortcomings and strengths. As I've already told you, one of my shortcomings in high school was not learning all I could from my classes and teachers. Your shortcoming may have been that you focused entirely on your studies without developing many outside interests. Someone else may feel that he concentrated so much on an outside activity—such as training for a particular sport—that he had no time for studies or friends. What was your major shortcoming in high school?

Now think about three things:

1. What pleased you in high school?
2. What could you have done better?
3. What do you want to improve upon in the future?

Identifying these areas will help you strike a good balance during college. Once you get in the habit of analyzing past experiences, you will have a clearer notion of what you do and don't want in the future. That's important.

As a high school senior, a college freshman or a college senior, the next thing you must do is decide to take action. Don't worry if you don't know what you want to do. Just commit yourself to the process.

If you do, you'll eventually find out which careers might be best for you and how you could best prepare for them.

RECAP: The priorities

1. Gain knowledge
2. Participate in activities
3. Get REAL-WORLD experience

Making It Happen

"Luck is the residue of design," said Branch Rickey, known as the baseball mahatma for his strategic methods for playing and organizing baseball. He developed the farm system on which the minor leagues were formed. His PLANS OF ACTION took a handful of disjointed teams in faraway cities and banded them into an organization which has left its mark on American culture.

Nothing happens magically. If you want to be a success, you are going to have to take personal responsibility for your life. Why do some graduates get twenty job offers and others receive none?

While successful people may appear lucky, they, in fact, illustrate the maxim that "luck favors the prepared mind." How do you arrange to have the most options when you leave college? Plan, develop foresight and take charge of your life and you will become one of the lucky ones. Most important, decide that you want to succeed—and believe it.

Charles Garfield, a clinical psychologist who has spent his career studying what motivates people to superior effort, says that the drive to excel comes primarily from within. Can "peak performances" be learned? Yes, says Garfield. High achievers are not extraordinarily gifted superhumans. What they have in common is the ability to cultivate what the German writer Johann Wolfgang von Goethe termed "the genius, power and magic" that exists in all of us. These doers increase the odds in their favor through simple techniques which anyone can cultivate:

1. Envision a mission
2. Be result-oriented
3. Tap your internal resources
4. Enlist team spirit
5. Treat setbacks as stepping stones

These are skills which this book is going to teach you.

First Things First

The first thing to keep in mind when planning: accept the world the way it is. Your plans should be based on a realistic assessment of how things are, not some starry-eyed vision of how they should be. You can dream, but there's a happy medium between cold reality and pie in the sky. That's why you must be open to opportunity. Indeed, you must create it. Although you can't change the hand you were dealt, you can play it as wisely as possible. That's what this book is about.

So start today. Start now.

The more questions you ask now, the better prepared you'll be in four years. You don't want to be stuck in a boring job or wondering why you can't find work.

Are you going to make mistakes? I hope so, unless you're not of the human species. Making mistakes is the process by which we learn. And whenever we're disappointed by the outcome, we have to maintain a positive attitude, log the information—and keep going. The key is to learn from mistakes without letting them slow us down.

·2·

DISCOVER WHO YOU ARE
Defining Your Interests, Abilities and Goals

Know thyself.
SOCRATES

To thine own self be true.
SHAKESPEARE

Phil was a pre-law freshman. After spending six months talking to law students and attorneys he made a great discovery: he realized that he didn't want to be a lawyer. No way, José. No area of law intrigued him. He disliked the hours of solitary research, and law didn't accommodate his strong suits—working with groups and developing programs. So Phil switched his major to English and his minor to history. Today he's in business for himself as an international marketing consultant. And he loves his work.

If you don't know yourself, you'll make uninformed decisions. My college friend Mary was an accounting major because she knew she'd be employable. She was right. However, after graduating she discovered that she hated working with numbers and, after just two years, quit accounting. So long, General Ledger.

I recently had dinner with Mary. She's living in New York and writing for *Connoisseur* magazine. We talked about the internal struggles that led to her career change. Now she's crazy about her job and only regrets that she didn't invest the time and energy in college to define her interests.

"College students shouldn't opt for a career because it will be easy

15

to find a job," Mary says. "Easy can equal uninteresting and unfulfilling if you don't have a passion for the work itself. Pursue that which will be rewarding in the short term AND the long term."

Cathy Hudnall agrees. After five years as a secretary at Wells, Fargo in San Francisco, she was invited to join the bank's junior officer training program. Realizing she had a true interest in and aptitude for banking, she enrolled in the American Graduate School of International Management. "Find out while you're in college what makes you tick," says Cathy, who is now a senior manager and vice president for Bank of Canada.

"Nothing great was ever achieved without enthusiasm," said Ralph Waldo Emerson. You want to be enthusiastic about your job. To do that, you must take some time to analyze what it is you like to do.

An honest and complete self-appraisal is your first step toward choosing the right career. By asking yourself critical questions, you'll be way ahead of most of your classmates. Leagues, fathoms, kilometers squared. WAY ahead.

The Three D's

Which of the following describes you best?

1. DRIFTER. Life just happens to you, often in ways decidedly unfriendly or random.
2. DREAMER. You have wonderful plans for the future but can't always realize your dreams. Your favorite line is borrowed from Scarlett O'Hara of *Gone With the Wind* fame: "I can't think about it now. I'll think about it tomorrow."
3. DOERS. You have the confidence, the vision and the persistence to make your goals come together. You plan, act and achieve.

Most people are some combination of the above. Maybe you've been a Drifter. In this chapter, you will graduate to Dreamer as you explore your interests, abilities and passions. The rest of the book is devoted to your becoming a Doer. Work hard and be patient.

Does this mean that drifting and dreaming are not important? On the contrary. One of my best friends, Madeline, aptly reminded me that a balance of drifting and dreaming is necessary. "All doing squashes the learning, pain and growth that dreaming and drifting inspire," she wrote. "Success is balance. It is reading well, thinking deeply, having the wisdom to see the broader picture, knowing the importance of friends and family."

A balance of drifting, dreaming and doing will help you define and achieve what you determine is most important in college, in work and in life.

So how might you go about "discovering" yourself? Here are four suggestions:

1. Keep a journal
2. Survey yourself
3. Keep asking questions
4. Overcome obstacles (mental and other)

1. Keep a Journal

Throughout college keep track of your plans, deeds, fears and dreams. Set down goals for yourself and then reread them after six months. Which have you achieved? Which do you want to pursue now?

Your journal is your secret companion. Write in it every day through good times and bad. Share your expectations and aspirations, your disappointments and fears. Write about the world as you see it. Be blunt. Be blatantly honest. After a month, begin rereading. Your journal will reveal interesting patterns. You'll see a definite progression, and that's rewarding.

2. Survey Yourself

Answer the following questions as honestly as you can. After all, no one else is going to see your answers. Remember that self-definition means figuring out both strengths and weaknesses. These questions should help you evaluate your high school experience and define your college goals.

Periodically, throughout your life, it's helpful to look back at what you've done so that you can get some perspective on what you want to do going forward. Later in the book you'll have a chance to look ahead and dream about what kinds of things you want to do. Now look back and reflect for a moment.

How I See Myself

1. In high school I felt most proud that I _____

2. I feel most disappointed that I did not _____

_____

3. The most important thing I learned was _____

_____

4. I developed confidence by _____

_____

5. The teacher who had the greatest positive influence on me was

_____ who taught me _____

_____

6. In high school I was motivated by _____

_____

_____

7. The five things I enjoyed most were _____

_____

8. The five things I enjoyed least were _____

_____

9. The five things I found most interesting were _____

_____

10. My biggest disappointment was _____

_____

11. My greatest success was _____

_____

12. The most difficult thing I've had to do was _____

_____

13. In high school I considered myself _____

_____

14. My friends would describe me as _____

15. I am often criticized for _____

_____

16. If I could change one thing in my life it would be _____

_____

17. I am angered by _____

18. I would describe myself as the kind of person who _____

_____

19. The thing I would most like to change about myself is _____

_____

20. My philosophy of life is _____

Myself Among Others

1. The kind of people I most like to be with are _____

_____

2. I most admire my fellow students and teachers who _____

_____

3. The kind of people I find it most difficult to be around are _____

_____

4. The person who has had the most influence on my life has been

_____

_____ because _____

_____

5. The character traits I most like in people are _____

_____

The ones I dislike most are _____

_____

6. Given the choice between being with others or by myself, I choose

to _____

_____ because _____

_____

Keep in mind that self-definition requires continual reexamination. As your perspective and ideas change, you'll find yourself revising your earlier lists. With each revision you move closer to your goals, both in the short and the long term. Don't worry if you can't answer all of these questions now. You'll have plenty of time in the next few years to explore several different areas which interest you. These answers will serve as your information base when the time comes to evaluate your career path.

3. Keep Asking Questions

Don't be complacent and accept everything you read and hear. Find out if things make sense. We've all read the slogan "Question Authority." Let it serve as a gentle reminder.

Challenge friends, parents and teachers in discussion. Learn opposing viewpoints and continually question your beliefs. Practice putting yourself in others' shoes. Continue to develop your critical thinking skills. Ask yourself what you're doing, why you're doing it and how you can do it better.

4. Overcome Obstacles (Mental and Other)

Everyone has insecurities and shortcomings. It's a fact of life. However, we don't usually like to explore our dark side. We keep it locked up tightly inside. Left unattended, our insecurities are manifested as fear. Rest assured that the more you try to run from fear, the more it will dominate your life. Be comforted by the fact that you do have a choice: you can be courageous and deal effectively with your fears.

What Do You Do?

The first step toward overcoming your fears is identifying them. Complete the following statements honestly.

1. Very few people realize that I am afraid _____

_____

2. When I am alone the thing that frightens me most is _____

_____

3. When I am with other people the thing that frightens me most is

_____

4. I'm embarrassed when _____

_____

5. My greatest fear about college is _____

The next step is to accept these fears. That's right. In order to overcome your fears it helps to embrace them.

Imagine that each of the five situations above came true and that you
were forced to confront your fear. Answer the following questions for
each: Describe the scene in detail. What happened? What does it feel
like? What are you thinking? What can you do to make the anxiety
more tolerable?

1. _____

_____

_____

2. _____

_____

_____

3. _____

_____

_____

4. _____

_____

_____

5. _____

_____

_____

Aside from fears, other obstacles will surely get in your way. Maybe you think you're not smart enough because of that IQ test you took in the fourth grade (you were having a bad day; it happens). Maybe you believe that you're incompetent because you didn't ace the SATs. Relax. Remember that Einstein flunked math in the eighth grade.

Einstein was not unique, at least not on that score. Bob Sternberg, a noted Yale psychologist, has done extensive research on IQ tests and intelligence. He has noted that intelligence is a composite of several factors. Many of these—including motivation and the capacity to adjust to change—can't be accurately measured by a written test.

If you do score well on aptitude tests, don't rest on your laurels. Your brain is not a bank. It cannot pay the rent; nor can it pay for the Himalayan odyssey you devised to get away from home for the summer. Stretch your natural talents by coupling your intellect with determination and a commitment to action.

There are other obstacles much more formidable than genius or the lack of it. Jackie Fitzgerald, the national sales manager for Sunlover Clothing Products, supported her family while attending Villanova University in Philadelphia. She began school as a pre-med student because her mother had always wanted her to be a doctor.

"I didn't have the financial support from my family that most students have. After I decided I didn't want to be a doctor, I lost all emotional support from my mom." This, Jackie says, was the greatest obstacle she had to overcome.

"Still, it's better to graduate with a solid education in a field you love than to pursue a career in an area you're not passionate about," Jackie says. With her many commitments, Jackie learned time management and self-reliance. She learned how to encourage herself when no one else was there to cheer her on. These skills enabled her to graduate with honors as a sociology major and psychology minor and to be enormously successful in business.

For Jill Goldfarb things were worse. As she began the first week of her freshman year at the University of Michigan, her mother died of a stroke. Jill dropped out of school for the fall semester, working at a department store before returning to Michigan in the spring. In March, her father died suddenly of a heart attack.

"I survived because I had to," says Jill, who immersed herself in her studies and extracurricular activities. Remarkably, Jill graduated with a 4.0 average and a degree in management information systems. Her hard work and dedication were perhaps the greatest tributes she could pay to her parents.

If you're starting college under difficult (or even tragic) circumstances, don't let a disadvantage deny you success. There is truth to the old adage that adversity breeds character. Learn the difference between situations that you can control and those that you can't. Set your sights on those that you can affect and then go for it.

Throughout life, each of us encounters obstacles and challenges on a regular basis. It's how we deal with these challenges, and what we make of them, that determines our true success.

·3·

FUTURES AND OPTIONS
Matching Your Interests
with a Career

I don't know what I'd like to do. That's what hurts the most. That's why I can't quit the job. I really don't know what talents I may have. And I don't know where to go to find out.

Chicago phone receptionist, in STUDS TERKEL, *Working*

There is a job, and a future, waiting for you, as long as you really want to work. There are opportunities galore, as long as you make the effort to seek them out. There are tested ways to success in the job market.

ROBERT O. SNELLING, SR., *The Right Job*

Rich man, poor man, beggar man, thief,
Doctor, lawyer, Indian chief . . .
CHILDREN'S NURSERY RHYME

Consider a typical freshman's noctural musings on what it means to use the career placement center:

A career placement center is a secret building in the middle of campus where seniors are escorted at night, blindfolded, for initiation into inescapable careers. Jobs are assigned on the basis of Alphabetical Synergy, a scientific technique developed in California during the mid-seventies. Alphabetical Synergy pairs career and candidate by matching the first letter of the student's last name with the first letter of a career.

EXAMPLE:

Michael Crosby: double major in economics and physics
Career Selected by Alphabetical Synergy: Coffey . . . CHEF . . . CRAPS PLAYER . . . no, wait a minute.
********CONTRACTOR********
!!!!!!!!!!!!!!!!!!!! !!!!!!!!!!!!!

25

Still blindfolded, Michael is given a burlap sack containing the tools of the trade: hammer, nails, hard hat and keys to the trailer which will be his new headquarters along with a map specifying its exact location at the construction site in Death Valley, California.

Then he wakes up, screaming.

The moral of this nightmare? Simple. Don't be afraid of your career placement center. It won't hurt you in the light of day. Don't wait until three days before graduation and expect to nail down the perfect job. Go early—during your freshman and sophomore years—to gather information about those fields which interest you. Placement centers have a wealth of materials, including books, company files, videos and names of contacts. Trained counselors are a valuable resource; they can help you get that summer internship, write your résumé, prepare for the interview, and lend an ear as you talk through job possibilities. *Take advantage of this service.*

Most placement centers offer interest surveys. Take them. They are a good place to begin to figure out what you want to do.

One such test, the Strong-Campbell Interest Inventory, compares student responses with those of professionals in various occupations. Students get an idea of the careers people with similar interests have chosen, pointing them toward jobs they may not have considered.

"But don't rely solely on standardized tests," says Tim Dalton, a senior at Columbia. "Many students who seek career guidance think they can just fill in the boxes, stick numbers into a computer and then get a printout on the career they should pursue. The tests are a starting place; you must look within yourself for the answers."

Sometimes these tests can be off target. Anne, a friend who is an editor, completed a survey which indicated that she could be a dental hygienist—a job in which she has no interest. Like a hygienist, however, Anne does enjoy working quietly by herself and with small groups of people. This is precisely what she does as an editor. The moral? Take survey results with a grain of salt. Consider the broader interest profile as well as the specific job suggestions.

Cyrus Vesser, who worked for twelve years before returning to school to get his doctorate in history, says that brainstorming helped him choose his career. "The self-assessment tests and group discussions provided by my university were useful," says Cyrus. "Five years of wrong leads can be avoided by self-examination and experimentation in areas which spark your mind."

Many students fear they won't get a job after graduation. They consider only a few of the thousands of possible professions from which to choose. Students who don't know what they want to do frequently accept jobs they hate or for which they're unsuited.

That's not how you want to spend your career—or your life. You can do better than that. Use your imagination! *There are thousands of jobs available.*

Your first step? *Relax.* You are going to get a job in the career of your choice. (Even if you now have no idea of what you want to do.)

Step Two: *Explore* the careers available to you—by reading, interviewing people, investigating your placement office. Find out how many options you really have.

Step Three: *Commit yourself* to the process of discovering what you want to do.

Step Four: *Chart* your career path(s) by listing:

1. Where you have been
2. What you have done
3. Where you are now
4. Where you want to go

Step Five: *Take action.*

Chapter 2 dealt with your past. Now let's focus on the present. In your journal, label a section "Personal Inventory Assessment" and devote at least one page to each of the following categories: interests; talents; skills; likes and dislikes; goals, values and ambitions. Don't worry if some of your answers don't make complete sense. Your thoughts will develop after you have a chance to reflect on your initial responses.

Interests

I am curious about

I question

I'm concerned about

I'm fascinated by

I like to think/read/write about

Talents

I am good at the following kinds of activities (physical, intellectual, creative, social, etc.)

People compliment me on

People encourage me to

Skills

(Specific skills such as public speaking, car maintenance, word processing, etc.)

Skills I have

Skills I want to learn

Likes and Dislikes

(About people—their character, habits, shortcomings, influence, etc.)

LIKES   DISLIKES

(About working environment—indoors or out, with people or alone, small company or large, etc.)

LIKES   DISLIKES

Goals, Values and Ambitions

I like

I want to accomplish

When I die I want to be remembered for

In life, I value these things most:

Contributions I want to make to the world:

Things that give me peace of mind:

After you've completed your self-assessment inventory, analyze your responses. Put a P next to each answer dealing with People. Put an I next to responses dealing with Ideas or Information. Put an O next to answers involving Objects. Now group the responses under the appropriate headings in the triangle below.

PEOPLE

INFORMATION   OBJECTS

Take a few minutes to consider the chart. What did you learn? Are there certain patterns? Clusters indicate a strong interest in that particular area. A group with few responses suggests the opposite.

You don't have to draw any conclusions now. The important thing is that you've identified your skills and interests.

What's so important about that? (You are not easily convinced.) What's important is that you can use this knowledge to choose career options. Many people spend years in unrewarding jobs before they realize that they are not utilizing their skills and interests. Consider the frequency of the mid-life crisis as evidence. You are learning a different path— and you haven't even graduated from college yet.

Ask the Right Questions

You have surveyed your skills and interests. You've analyzed whether you work best with people, information or objects. Now it's time to examine the specific characteristics of different career options. On pages 36–49 is a reprint of "The World of Work: A Sampler" from *What Color Is Your Parachute?* by Richard Bolles.

The chart is divided into professions. The job requirements are listed across the top. Which of these characteristics describe you? Consider which professions interest you. What training would you need in the next four years to prepare yourself?

Now consider the work environment category. Are these the conditions under which you work best? If not, what adjustments would you have to make? How difficult or easy would these adjustments be?

What about the occupational characteristics? Are there plenty of jobs in your areas of interest? Will your prospective industry grow over the next few years?

Consider these questions as you read the next few pages. Remember, you don't have to decide anything now. All you need to do is start a running list of four or five areas you might be interested in. Over the next few years you'll explore them and choose your career.

Learn to Reason

Why do we accept what we believe? It's important to understand the underlying motives and logic of our beliefs. Lex Kaplan began college thinking that he wanted to be a lawyer. Originally from Englewood, New Jersey, Lex majored in journalism. As president of his college political magazine he "fell in love" with reporting and writing. He enjoyed it so much that he freelanced for *The Phoenix*, a Boston periodical, when he graduated. He used his writing experience there to help him land a job at *The New Yorker*, fact checking and writing "Talk of the Town" pieces. But after a year he feared that being a journalist would make him a dilettante—a writer without a specialty. So, without reasoning, he reverted to his pre-freshman beliefs and enrolled in law school. He quickly realized his mistake. While he was a hard worker, having earned a B.A. in history and literature, he discovered something about himself at law school.

"I found out I wasn't a fighter," he says. Competition on campus for corporate jobs was fierce. Lex found himself disliking both the competition and the idea of corporate law, which to him "seemed like a form of death." This time Lex used his experiences in making his next career move. He turned down a job with a law firm in New York and combined all his skills in starting up his own magazine.

Once you've made up your mind, get used to defending your opinion both orally and in writing. Throughout your college and working career, you will continually have to (1) come up with your own ideas and (2) convince others of their validity.

Lex did exactly that. He came up with a novel idea for a magazine that would fill a void in the market. He gave a seven-page proposal to an acquaintance he knew was interested in investing in the arts and the man gave him $50,000. For the next year Lex enthusiastically pitched his concept to authors, friends and investors. Within that year he convinced some *New Yorker* staffers to switch to his magazine (called *Wigwag*), contracted articles from known authors, including Alice McDermott, Ralph Ellison and Richard Ford, and raised $3 million. All this he did from his two-bedroom apartment in New York, making the most of his "cold" phone calls and "blind" visits. Because Lex Kaplan believed in his project, many others did too.

Dream On

Now that you've defined your interests, skills and goals, it's time to focus on the job that will incorporate them. What would you like to do if you could do anything? Really, truly, outlandishly . . . *anything*. Imagine the sheer delight of finding the career that taps your passion and allows you the privilege of being paid for doing it! Now you are going to do just that. Using the insights you gained from the inventory, design your own success story. Where do you work? Does your job include travel? What is an average day like? What is your compensation? (Does this include your quarterly bonus?) Describe your position in detail. The goal is to make it real. Try to taste it, hear it, feel it. Do not hold back. *Write it down.*

Dream-Boat Job/Stellar Achievement #1

Dream-Boat Job/Stellar Achievement #2

Dream-Boat Job/Stellar Achievement #3

Putting It All Together

It's time to take your head out of the clouds and focus on strategies that will make these dreams become reality.

The Narrowing Process

Once you've analyzed the bigger picture, pick two or three areas of interest and begin developing career strategies for each. Write them down below. (If you don't know yet, come back to this after you've had more time to think.)

Using What You Know

The key to choosing career options is a willingness to explore. You could convert the basics of the above approach to fit any possible path: poet, advertising copywriter, stockbroker, farmer, cowboy or corporate psychic. Remember, you're interested in these careers (all of them) because you think they would be fun. So have fun finding out.

And while you're out pioneering, continue to ask yourself questions that will help to refine your career goals:

1. How can I gather more information about those careers which interest me?
2. Whom do I know in this field? (If you don't know anyone, find out whom you can meet.) What can they tell me about this area? What specific questions will I ask them?
3. What else can I do each week and each month to prepare myself? Remember that experience leads to intelligent decisions.

Career Goals

"Your job becomes your lifestyle," says Tony Ponturo, director of media services for Anheuser-Busch. "So you'd better like what you're doing."

Tony is right. Know what you want even if you don't know how to get it right now. The path to a really interesting career is not always direct.

After college Tony identified the three areas he loved most—business, sports and television. He moved to New York City and got a job as a page for NBC, hoping to get a foot in the door of NBC Sports. That didn't work. So he took an alternate route and went into advertising, working for three successive advertising agencies as a media buyer. His work on a Coca-Cola campaign earned him a shot at his firm's Budweiser account. Anheuser-Busch was so impressed with his work that they lured him away from the agency and created a position for him in their home office in St. Louis. Since Busch promotes heavily on sports telecasts, Tony finds himself working in all three of the areas he enjoys: business, sports and television (and then there's the beer!).

Larry Maslon got his job through a similarly circuitous route. Larry is the dramaturge for the prestigious Arena Stage in Washington, D.C. He helps to choose the season's repertoire, interprets the plays, researches their historical background and edits the theater's publications. But when he started out, Larry knew nothing of dramaturgy—he only knew what he liked. A lover of directing and Renaissance literature, he majored in both in college. For his final project in theater arts he directed *The Tempest* and then wrote a paper on the play for his Renaissance literature thesis.

"Unbeknownst to me," says Larry, "by both critically examining and producing a play, I was doing a dramaturge's work." Later, intending to become a theater director, he enrolled in a master's program in theater arts at Stanford. He was disappointed that the program focused primarily on the academic side of theater, so he directed some plays on his own time.

"Again unbeknownst to me, I was becoming exquisitely prepared to be a dramaturge," he says. He now possesses something that is extremely rare: a challenging, steady job in the theater. Larry strongly advocates that every student pursue what he or she loves. He says he has benefited from following his heart, from doing what he's done "in spite of myself."

Malcolm Forbes, publisher of *Forbes* magazine, says in *The Achievement Factors*, by B. Eugene Griessman, "I think the foremost quality—there's no success without it—is really loving what you do. If you love it, you will do it well."

"You've got to have fire in the gut," says Milton Pedraza, a recruiter and marketer for Colgate (the company, not the college). "You have to be committed to your job once you land it, but in college you must commit yourself to becoming as well educated and well prepared as possible, even if you don't yet know what kind of work interests you." If you don't develop a burning passion to get things done in college, Milton says, it will be hard to motivate yourself on the job.

Setting Your Goals

Your senior year, though it seems a long way off, is just around the corner. The trick of not being caught off guard by its arrival is balance: balancing the long term with current agendas for the month, the week, the day, the moment. For now (this moment) set some career goals. Don't worry about revising them. That will come later. Time is very forgiving to those who act, which is what you're doing by committing to a career direction . . . however tentative.

Your career direction will find its shape, and its name, in increments. Everything you study and explore now will contribute to the résumé you put together during your senior year. It will summarize the whole shebang—academic achievements, extracurricular activities and work experience.

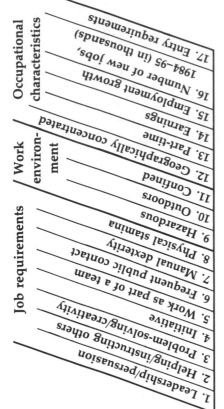

The World of Work: A Sampler

	Job requirements											Work environment			Occupational characteristics		
	1. Leadership/persuasion	2. Helping/instructing others	3. Problem-solving/creativity	4. Initiative	5. Work as part of a team	6. Frequent public contact	7. Manual dexterity	8. Physical stamina	9. Hazardous	10. Outdoors	11. Confined	12. Geographically concentrated	13. Part-time	14. Earnings	15. Employment growth	16. Number of new jobs, 1984–95 (in thousands)	17. Entry requirements
Executive, Administrative & Managerial Occupations																	
Managers & Administrators																	
Bank officers & managers	•	•	•	•	•					•				H	H	119	H
Health services managers	•	•	•	•	•									H	H	147	H
Hotel managers & assistants	•	•	•	•	•									(1)	H	21	M
School principals & assistant principals	•	•	•	•	•									H	L	12	H
Management Support Occupations																	
Accountants & auditors	•	•	•	•						•				H	H	307	H
Construction & building inspectors			•	•	•	•			•	•				M	L	4	M
Inspectors & compliance officers, except construction			•	•	•	•			•	•				H	L	10	M
Personnel, Training & Labor Relations Specialists																	
Purchasing agents	•	•	•	•	•									H	M	34	H
Underwriters		•	•	•										H	H	36	H
Wholesale & retail buyers	•	•	•	•										H	H	17	H
														M	M	28	H

Engineers, Surveyors & Architects

Architects	H	H	25	H
Surveyors	M	M	6	M
Engineers				
Aerospace engineers	H	H	14	H
Chemical engineers	H	H	13	H
Civil engineers	H	H	46	H
Electrical & electronics engineers	H	H	206	H
Industrial engineers	H	H	37	H
Mechanical engineers	H	H	81	H
Metallurgical, ceramics & materials engineers	H	H	4	H
Mining engineers	H	L	(2)	H
Nuclear engineers	H	L	1	H
Petroleum engineers	H	M	4	H

1. Estimates not available.

2. Less than 500.

L = Lowest   M = Middle   H = Highest

From *Occupational Outlook Quarterly*, Vol. 30, No. 3 (Fall 1986)

Natural Scientists & Mathematicians

	Job requirements											Work environment		Occupational characteristics			
	1. Leadership/persuasion	2. Helping/instructing others	3. Problem-solving/creativity	4. Initiative	5. Work as part of a team	6. Frequent public contact	7. Manual dexterity	8. Physical stamina	9. Hazardous	10. Outdoors	11. Confined	12. Geographically concentrated	13. Part-time	14. Earnings	15. Employment growth	16. Number of new jobs, 1984–95 (in thousands)	17. Entry requirements
Computer & Mathematical Occupations																	
Actuaries		•	•								•			H	H	4	H
Computer systems analysts	•	•	•	•							•			H	H	212	H
Mathematicians		•	•											H	M	4	H
Statisticians		•	•											H	M	4	H
Physical Scientists																	
Chemists		•	•											H	L	9	H
Geologists & geophysicists		•	•	•					•	•				H	M	7	H
Meteorologists		•	•	•										H	M	1	H
Physicists & astronomers		•	•											H	L	2	H
Life Scientists																	
Agricultural scientists		•	•											(1)	M	3	H
Biological scientists		•	•											H	M	10	H
Foresters & conservation scientists	•	•	•	•			•	•	•					H	L	2	H

Social Scientists, Social Workers, Religious Workers & Lawyers

Occupation			
Lawyers	H H	174	H
Social Scientists & Urban Planners			
Economists	H M	7	H
Psychologists	H H	21	H
Sociologists	H L	(2)	H
Urban & regional planners	H L	2	H
Social & Recreation Workers			
Social workers	M H	75	H
Recreation workers	L H	25	M
Religious Workers			
Protestant ministers	L	(1)	H
Rabbis	H	(1)	H
Roman Catholic priests	L	(1)	H

Teachers, Counselors, Librarians & Archivists

Occupation			
Kindergarten & elementary school teachers	M H	281	H
Secondary school teachers	M L	43	H
Adult & vocational education teachers	M M	43	H
College & university faculty	H L	-77	H
Counselors	M M	29	H
Librarians	M L	16	H
Archivists & curators	M L	1	H

Health Diagnosing & Treating Practitioners

Occupation	Job requirements									Work environment				Occupational characteristics			
	1. Leadership/persuasion	2. Helping/instructing others	3. Problem-solving/creativity	4. Initiative	5. Work as part of a team	6. Frequent public contact	7. Manual dexterity	8. Physical stamina	9. Hazardous	10. Outdoors	11. Confined	12. Geographically concentrated	13. Part-time	14. Earnings	15. Employment Growth	16. Number of new jobs, 1984–95 (in thousands)	17. Entry requirements
Chiropractors	•	•	•	•	•	•								H	H	9	H
Dentists	•	•	•	•	•	•								H	H	39	H
Optometrists	•	•	•	•	•	•								H	H	8	H
Physicians	•	•	•	•	•	•						•		H	H	109	H
Podiatrists	•	•	•	•	•	•								H	H	4	H
Veterinarians	•	•	•	•	•	•	•	•						H	H	9	H

Registered Nurses, Pharmacists, Dietitians, Therapists & Physician Assistants

Occupation	Job requirements									Work environment				Occupational characteristics			
	1. Leadership/persuasion	2. Helping/instructing others	3. Problem-solving/creativity	4. Initiative	5. Work as part of a team	6. Frequent public contact	7. Manual dexterity	8. Physical stamina	9. Hazardous	10. Outdoors	11. Confined	12. Geographically concentrated	13. Part-time	14. Earnings	15. Employment Growth	16. Number of new jobs, 1984–95 (in thousands)	17. Entry requirements
Dietitians & nutritionists	•	•	•	•	•	•								M	H	12	H
Occupational therapists		•	•	•	•	•	•							(1)	H	8	H
Pharmacists	•	•	•	•	•					•				H	L	15	H
Physical therapists	•	•	•	•	•	•	•							M	H	25	H
Physician assistants	•	•	•	•	•	•	•							M	H	10	M

Recreational therapists	•	•		•	•	•	•	•	•		•				M	H	4	M
Registered nurses	•	•		•	•	•	•	•	•	•	•			•	M	H	452	M
Respiratory therapists	•	•		•	•		•	•		•					M	H	11	L
Speech pathologists & audiologists	•	•		•	•		•								M	M	8	H

Health Technologists & Technicians

Clinical laboratory technologists & technicians		•			•	•	•				•			L	L	18	(3)
Dental hygienists		•		•	•	•	•						•	L	H	22	M
Dispensing opticians		•		•	•	•	•							M	H	10	M
Electrocardiograph technicians		•		•	•	•	•							(1)	M	5	M
Electroenceph. technologists & technicians		•		•	•	•	•			•				(1)	H	1	M
Emergency medical technicians	•	•		•	•	•	•							L	L	3	M
Licensed practical nurses		•		•	•	•	•							L	M	106	M
Medical record technicians			•	•	•							•		L	H	10	M
Radiologic technologists		•		•	•	•	•							L	H	27	M
Surgical technicians		•		•	•	•	•							L	M	5	M

Writers, Artists & Entertainers

	1. Leadership/persuasion	2. Helping/instructing others	3. Problem-solving/creativity	4. Initiative	5. Work as part of a team	6. Frequent public contact	7. Manual dexterity	8. Physical stamina	9. Hazardous	10. Outdoors	11. Confined	12. Geographically concentrated	13. Part-time	14. Earnings	15. Employment Growth	16. Number of new jobs, 1984–95 (in thousands)	17. Entry requirements
	Job requirements									Work environment					Occupational characteristics		
Communications Occupations																	
Public relations specialists	•		•	•	•	•								H	H	30	H
Radio & TV announcers & newscasters	•	•	•	•	•	•				•				L	M	6	H
Reporters & correspondents	•		•	•	•									(1)	M	13	H
Writers & editors	•		•	•						•		•		(1)	H	54	H
Visual Arts Occupations																	
Designers			•	•	•		•							H	H	46	H
Graphic & fine artists			•	•	•		•								H	60	M
Photographers & camera operators			•	•	•		•					•		M	H	29	M
Performing Arts Occupations																	
Actors, directors & producers			•	•	•	•					•	•		L	H	11	M
Dancers & choreographers			•	•	•	•	•	•			•	•		L	H	2	M
Musicians			•	•	•	•	•					•		L	M	26	M

Technologists & Technicians, Except Health

Engineering & Science Technicians

Occupation			
Drafters	M M	39	M
Electrical & electronics technicians	M H	202	M
Engineering technicians	M H	90	M
Science technicians	M M	40	M

Other Technicians

Occupation			
Air traffic controllers	H L	(2)	H
Broadcast technicians	M H	5	M
Computer programmers	H H	245	H
Legal assistants	M H	51	L
Library technicians	L L	4	L
Tool programmers, numerical control	M H	3	M

Marketing & Sales Occupations

Occupation			
Cashiers	L H	566	L
Insurance sales workers	M L	34	M
Manufacturers' sales workers	H L	51	H
Real estate agents & brokers	M M	52	M
Retail sales workers	L M	583	L
Securities & financial services sales workers	H H	32	H
Travel agents	(1) H	32	M
Wholesale trade sales workers	M H	369	M

Administrative Support Occupations, Including Clerical

Occupation	Job requirements									Work environment				Occupational characteristics			
	1. Leadership/persuasion	2. Helping/instructing others	3. Problem-solving/creativity	4. Initiative	5. Work as part of a team	6. Frequent public contact	7. Manual dexterity	8. Physical stamina	9. Hazardous	10. Outdoors	11. Confined	12. Geographically concentrated	13. Part-time	14. Earnings	15. Employment growth	16. Number of new jobs, 1984–95 (in thousands)	17. Entry requirements
Bank tellers				•	•						•	•	•	L	L	24	L
Bookkeepers & accounting clerks		•		•							•	•	•	L	L	118	L
Computer & peripheral equipment operators		•		•	•						•			L	H	143	M
Data entry keyers				•	•		•				•			L	L	10	L
Mail carriers					•	•		•	•	•				M	L	8	L
Postal clerks					•	•	•			•				M	L	−27	L
Receptionists & information clerks	•			•	•	•					•	•		L	M	83	L
Reservation & transportation ticket agents & travel clerks	•	•		•	•	•				•		•		M	L	7	L
Secretaries	•		•	•	•	•					•			L	L	268	L
Statistical clerks			•	•	•					•				L	L	−12	L
Stenographers			•	•						•				L	L	−96	L
Teacher aides	•	•		•	•	•						•		L	M	88	L
Telephone operators	•	•		•	•					•				L	M	89	L
Traffic, shipping & receiving clerks			•	•						•				L	L	61	L
Typists				•			•				•		•	L	L	11	L

Service Occupations

Protective Service Occupations

Occupation				
Correction officers	M	H	45	L
Firefighting occupations	M	M	48	L
Guards	L	H	188	L
Police & detectives	M	M	66	L

Food & Bev. Preparation & Serv. Occupations

Occupation				
Bartenders	L	H	112	M
Chefs & cooks except short order	L	H	210	M
Waiters & waitresses	L	H	424	L

Health Service Occupations

Occupation				
Dental assistants	L	H	48	L
Medical assistants	L	H	79	L
Nursing aides	L	H	348	L
Psychiatric aides	L	L	5	L

Cleaning Service Occupations

Occupation				
Janitors & cleaners	L	M	443	L

Personal Service Occupations

Occupation				
Barbers	L	L	4	M
Childcare workers	L	L	55	L
Cosmetologists & related workers	L	H	150	M
Flight attendants	M	H	13	L

Agricultural, Forestry & Fishing Occupations

Occupation				
Farm operators & managers	M	L	-62	L

Mechanics & Repairers

Occupation	1. Leadership/persuasion	2. Helping/instructing others	3. Problem-solving/creativity	4. Initiative	5. Work as part of a team	6. Frequent public contact	7. Manual dexterity	8. Physical stamina	9. Hazardous	10. Outdoors	11. Confined	12. Geographically concentrated	13. Part-time	14. Earnings	15. Employment Growth	16. Number of new jobs, 1984-95 (in thousands)	17. Entry requirements
Vehicle & Mobile Equip. Mechanics & Repairers																	
Aircraft mechanics & engine specialists		•		•			•	•	•		•	•		H	M	18	M
Automotive & motorcycle mechanics		•			•	•	•	•		•				M	H	185	M
Automotive body repairers		•					•	•		•				M	M	32	M
Diesel mechanics							•	•		•				M	H	48	M
Farm equipment mechanics		•					•	•	•					M	L	2	M
Mobile heavy equipment mechanics		•					•	•		•				M	M	12	M
Electrical & Electronic Equipment Repairers																	
Commercial & electronic equipment repairers		•	•		•	•	•							L	M	8	M
Communications equipment mechanics		•	•		•	•	•							M	L	3	M
Computer service technicians		•	•		•	•	•	•						M	H	28	M
Electronic home entertainment equip. repairers		•	•			•	•	•				•		M	M	7	M
Home appliance & power tool repairers		•	•			•	•							L	M	9	M
Line installers & cable splicers		•					•	•	•					M	M	24	L

Occupation																
Telephone installers & repairers						•	•		•			M	L	−19	L
Other Mechanics & Repairers																
General maintenance mechanics	•					•					•	M	M	137	M
Heating, air-cond. & refrig. mechanics	•					•	•		•		•	M	M	29	M
Industrial machinery repairers	•					•	•		•		•	M	L	34	M
Millwrights						•	•		•		•	H	L	6	M
Musical instrument repairers & tuners									•		•	L	L	1	M
Office machine & cash register servicers	•	•							•		•	M	H	15	M
Vending machine servicers & repairers	•	•				•			•		•	(1)	M	5	M
Construction & Extractive Occupations																
Construction Occupations																
Bricklayers & stonemasons	•					•	•		•		•	M	M	15	M
Carpenters	•				•	•	•		•		•	M	M	101	M
Carpet installers	•			•		•	•		•		•	M	M	11	M
Concrete masons & terrazzo workers	•				•	•	•		•		•	M	M	17	M
Drywall workers & lathers	•				•	•	•		•		•	M	M	11	M
Electricians	•					•	•		•		•	H	M	88	M
Glaziers	•				•	•	•		•		•	M	H	8	M
Insulation workers	•				•	•	•		•		•	M	M	7	M
Painters & paperhangers	•			•		•	•		•		•	M	L	17	M
Plasterers	•		•			•	•		•		•	M	L	1	M
Plumbers & pipefitters	•					•	•		•		•	H	M	61	M
Roofers	•					•	•		•		•	L	M	16	M

Construction & Extractive Occupations (continued)

	Job requirements											Work environment			Occupational characteristics		
	1. Leadership/persuasion	2. Helping/instructing others	3. Problem-solving/creativity	4. Initiative	5. Work as part of a team	6. Frequent public contact	7. Manual dexterity	8. Physical stamina	9. Hazardous	10. Outdoors	11. Confined	12. Geographically concentrated	13. Part-time	14. Earnings	15. Employment growth	16. Number of new jobs, 1984–95 (in thousands)	17. Entry requirements
Sheet-metal workers		•		•			•	•						M	M	16	M
Structural & reinforcing metal workers		•		•			•	•	•					H	M	16	M
Tilesetters		•					•							M	M	3	M
Extractive Occupations																	
Roustabouts				•			•	•	•		•			M	L	(2)	L
Production Occupations																	
Blue-collar worker supervisors	•		•			•	•	•						M	L	85	M
Precision Production Occupations																	
Boilermakers		•				•	•	•	•	•				M	L	4	M
Bookbinding workers	•					•	•	•		•				L	M	14	M
Butchers and meatcutters					•	•	•	•		•				L	L	−9	M
Compositors & typesetters						•	•							L	M	14	M
Dental laboratory technicians							•			•				L	M	10	M
Jewelers	•	•	•	•		•	•			•	•			L	L	3	M

Occupation				
Lithographic & photoengraving workers	H	M	13	M
Machinists	M	L	37	M
Photographic process workers	L	H	14	L
Shoe & leather workers & repairers	L	L	−8	M
Tool-and-die makers	H	L	16	M
Upholsterers	L	L	6	M
Plant & System Operators				
Stationary engineers	M	L	4	M
Water & sewage treatment plant operators	L	M	10	M
Machine Operators, Tenders & Setup Workers				
Metalworking & plastic-working mach. operators	L	L	3	L
Numerical-control machine-tool operators	M	H	17	M
Printing press operators	M	M	26	M
Fabricators, Assemblers & Handworkg. Occup.				
Precision assemblers	L	M	66	L
Transportation equipment painters	M	M	9	M
Welders & cutters	M	M	41	M
Transportation & Material Moving Occupations				
Aircraft pilots	H	H	13	M
Busdrivers	M	M	77	M
Construction machinery operators	M	M	32	M
Industrial truck & tractor operators	M	L	−46	M
Truckdrivers	M	M	428	M
Handlers, Equip. Cleaners, Helpers & Laborers				
Construction trades helpers	L	L	27	L

Building Your Résumé

It can be done. Below are the résumés of some recent college grads. Note that each clearly identifies achievement in the three areas: academic, extracurricular and work experience. Your résumé should do the same. It should reflect what you've accomplished over your four years in college.

Robert Sánchez

Permanent Address

552 Rowe Street
Beach Harbor, CA 16589
(304) 952-8967

Education

University of San Diego
Bachelor of Arts, 1990
Major coursework:
Political science, public policy study
GPA: 3.4/4.0

Experience

Tutor—Double Discovery Center
Tutored economically and socially disadvantaged high school students in geometry and algebra.

Salesman/Clerk—Oberlin Outlets
Assisted in sales and marketing of retail furniture.

Assistant Librarian—Putnam Publishing
Maintained reference library for several professional magazines.

Assistant

Congressman Joseph Addabbo
Worked on re-election campaign in a door-to-door survey and at the registration station.

Volunteer Work

Advisor—Planned recreational activities for "Big Brother" program.

Teacher—Taught weekly Spanish lessons to elementary school class as part of high school outreach program.

Personal

Three-year pitcher/second baseman for USD Baseball Team
Mariette High School Humanitarian Award (1986)

References available upon request.

Sophie Chen

Current Address   *Permanent Address*

989 College Station   4 Highland Avenue
University of Illinois   Dallas, Texas 87609
Urbana, Ill. 89769

OBJECTIVE: Entry level position in engineering with op-
                         portunities in business and management.

EDUCATION: University of Illinois
                         School of Engineering and Applied Sciences
                         Candidate for Bachelor of Science, May 1990
                         Major: Industrial Engineering
                         GPA: 3.3/4.0

ACADEMIC HONORS: U of Ill. Engineering Prentis Scholar
                         AT&T Scholarship 1988–1990
                         Blue Lion Scholarship
                         Who's Who Among Students in American
                         Universities

EXPERIENCE:
Summer 1989   The Massachusetts Advanced Studies Pro-
                         gram
                         Teaching Intern
                         —Worked closely with bright high school
                          juniors.
                         —Assisted teaching advanced topics in math-
                          ematics; linear algebra, probability.
                         —Led recreational and educational field trips.

8/89–12/89   Johnson & Johnson, New Brunswick, NJ
                         General Assistant
                         —Documented and verified all transactions
                          for over 300 clients.
                         —Confirmed stock holdings for computer and
                          paper accounts.
                         —Organized and filed financial reports.

| Summer 1987 1988 | Arco Mounting Company, Dallas, Texas Engineering and Sales Assistant —Designed a more efficient factory layout. —Performed work sampling and cost analysis. —Negotiated sales with customers. —Created mechanical drawings of vibration isolators. |

ACTIVITIES: President, Engineering Junior Class.
                         Captain, Intercollegiate Volleyball Team.

William R. Woodard

Permanent Residence   *School Residence*

67 Sawmill Lane   Lambda Chi Alpha
Columbia, SC 93543   306 Church Street
(803) 444-8919   Norman, OK 55903
                                   (801) 343-1222

CAREER OBJECTIVE:

To obtain an entry level position in the financial division of a corporate firm that will eventually lead to a managerial position.

EDUCATION:

University of Oklahoma
B.A., economics

EXPERIENCE:

Summers

1988–89   AT&T Technology-Financial Planning and Analysis Division.
            Special Technology Assistant and Assistant to the Financial Planner. Created a computer-generated form for clientele, self-taught computer programming, interrelationary assignments with production items, word processing, computer programming and spreadsheet development for detailed analysis of billing and procedures, customer relations with other headquarters for significant information, data entry during price changes or additions.

1988   Hollings and Lombard—Accounting and Personnel. Assistant to the Personnel and Accounting Directors. Met and assisted new auditors and trainees, handled cash flow in the accounting department, handled insurance forms for auditors and staff, relief duties for project overflow.

COMPUTER KNOWLEDGE:

Symphony, Multimate, Lotus 1-2-3, and MS DOS.

ACTIVITIES:

Inroads Intern, Inroads, OK. May 1989 to present. Internship based on attendance at mandatory workshops and seminars in business communications, decision-making, time management, leadership styles, financial management and personnel management skills.

Black Students' Organization

The Bombshell Résumé

We've established that most students resist résumés for as long as they possibly can, usually until the second semester of their senior year. While this procrastination is understandable, it is not, in most cases, helpful in finding a job. Wait until the second semester of your senior year and you may find yourself distributing political tracts at the local mall—for the opposition party at minimum wage.

So why tempt Fate when it is so easily outfoxed? Start thinking about how you'd like your résumé to look now. Can't picture it? Turn the page and write it out.

My Dream Résumé

(By the second semester of my senior year)

My grade point average is _____

My major and minor are ⎯⎯⎯⎯⎯⎯⎯⎯⎯⎯⎯⎯⎯⎯⎯⎯⎯⎯⎯⎯⎯⎯

My career goal is ⎯⎯⎯⎯⎯⎯⎯⎯⎯⎯⎯⎯⎯⎯⎯⎯⎯⎯⎯⎯⎯⎯⎯⎯

⎯⎯⎯⎯⎯⎯⎯⎯⎯⎯⎯⎯⎯⎯⎯⎯⎯⎯⎯⎯⎯⎯⎯⎯⎯⎯⎯⎯⎯⎯⎯⎯⎯⎯⎯⎯

My academic honors include ⎯⎯⎯⎯⎯⎯⎯⎯⎯⎯⎯⎯⎯⎯⎯⎯⎯⎯

⎯⎯⎯⎯⎯⎯⎯⎯⎯⎯⎯⎯⎯⎯⎯⎯⎯⎯⎯⎯⎯⎯⎯⎯⎯⎯⎯⎯⎯⎯⎯⎯⎯⎯⎯⎯

⎯⎯⎯⎯⎯⎯⎯⎯⎯⎯⎯⎯⎯⎯⎯⎯⎯⎯⎯⎯⎯⎯⎯⎯⎯⎯⎯⎯⎯⎯⎯⎯⎯⎯⎯⎯

My extracurricular activities include ⎯⎯⎯⎯⎯⎯⎯⎯⎯⎯⎯⎯

⎯⎯⎯⎯⎯⎯⎯⎯⎯⎯⎯⎯⎯⎯⎯⎯⎯⎯⎯⎯⎯⎯⎯⎯⎯⎯⎯⎯⎯⎯⎯⎯⎯⎯⎯⎯

⎯⎯⎯⎯⎯⎯⎯⎯⎯⎯⎯⎯⎯⎯⎯⎯⎯⎯⎯⎯⎯⎯⎯⎯⎯⎯⎯⎯⎯⎯⎯⎯⎯⎯⎯⎯

I had a summer internship doing ⎯⎯⎯⎯⎯⎯⎯⎯⎯⎯⎯⎯⎯⎯⎯

at ⎯⎯⎯⎯⎯⎯⎯⎯⎯⎯⎯⎯⎯⎯⎯⎯⎯⎯⎯⎯⎯⎯⎯⎯⎯⎯⎯⎯⎯⎯⎯⎯⎯⎯

I traveled to ⎯⎯⎯⎯⎯⎯⎯⎯⎯⎯⎯⎯⎯⎯⎯⎯⎯⎯⎯⎯⎯⎯⎯⎯⎯⎯⎯

I worked part-time as _____

_____

My references are: 1. _____

2. _____

3. _____

Getting Started on the Road to Stockholm

To materialize the Dream Résumé (and not just on paper) you'll have to learn how to plan. That's not as easy as it seems, but don't despair. Planning can be learned.

First, distinguish between projection and planning. Projection usually comes first. It entails dreaming about what you want, including the soon to be realized fantasy of your acceptance speech, in Stockholm, when you humbly thank the world for that long-deserved prize (you are thirty-three before the committee finally comes to its stuffed-up senses and has the decency to recognize you). But envisioning the goal is not enough.

Once you've visualized the epic ending, you have to figure HOW to get there. The how requires creativity, tenacity and—most vexing—discipline. You will not automatically become a chief executive officer, no matter how potent your powers of fantasy. It takes 1 percent inspiration and vision coupled with 99 percent perspiration and hard work.

It is your task to map out the road to the corner office or mid-office cubicle or outdoor post—from college classes, internships, work experience and appropriate role models. Remember to take it one step at a time: 100,000 planned steps will go by much more quickly than 100,000 unplanned steps.

Below is a list of *broad* goals a college student might realistically expect to accomplish. (Notice I said "a" college student, as in *any* college student but not necessarily *all* college students.) If, in your considered opinion, this agenda doesn't suit the Road to Stockholm, fine. Come up with one that does. As your career adviser, I only make suggestions. You make the decisions.

Freshman Year Objectives

1. Assess your study skills and habits; improve on them if they need work
2. Get off to a good start academically
3. Apply for a second semester or summer part-time job
4. Join at least one extracurricular activity
5. Adjust to the responsibility of your new environment
6. Have fun

Sophomore Year Objectives

1. Apply for several summer internships
2. Begin planning your junior summer, semester or year abroad
3. Make at least one career contact
4. Join one or two clubs or special-interest groups
5. Continue to make good grades and get the most out of your classes
6. Cultivate mentors (see Chapter 8)
7. Register with the placement office
8. Have fun

Junior Year Objectives

1. Spend the summer, semester or year abroad
2. Plan an internship between your junior and senior years
3. Join another activity or honorary
4. Mail out preliminary job inquiry letters
5. Become a leader of one of the organizations you've joined
6. Prepare your résumé
7. Take some classes which don't pertain to your major but which will make you a well-qualified job applicant and a more interesting person
8. Have fun

Senior Year Objectives

1. Wage full-fledged job search in early fall
2. Make many business contacts; gather information
3. Send out at least twenty-five cover letters with résumés

4. Research the companies with whom you wish to interview

5. Have mock interviews to prepare for the real thing

6. Land the job, negotiate your salary and start taking home a paycheck

7. Have fun

Look at the list closely. See how a freshman year job helped land a sophomore year internship? That's the idea: one year's accomplishments increase the next year's options.

Should you aim to do all these things? Probably not. Choose those activities which suit you best and be proud of yourself for trying new things and having the vision to plan for the bigger picture.

Don't forget the common thread that ties each year together—*having fun!*

As you plan, scheme and connive on behalf of your noble destiny, keep in mind the three areas you'll need to develop: academic, extra-curricular and work experience.

Academic

solid education
good grades

EXTRACURRICULAR

travel

volunteer/community service

WORK

part-time jobs

work-study internships

Strive for balance. Keep this triangle in focus—maybe it won't be equilateral; just make sure it's got three sides.

Log the specific steps you think you'll have to take to get from where you are to where you want to be. The rest of this book will help you take the steps . . . one at a time.

The Game of Destiny Plan

Freshman Year

Sophomore Year

Junior Year

Senior Year

The First Five Steps

Still tempted to pole-vault to glory? Resist. Below are five steps designed to assure achievement on the Road to Stockholm, Podunk, El Lay, Boise or wherever it is you want to go. Keep them handy for encouragement.

1. Strike a Balance

"Learn to balance things," says Jeff Rosenthal, who landed a job with IBM upon graduation. In college, you'll have to balance your academic, personal and real-world experience. Make good grades but realize that good grades alone are usually not enough. (Even if you want to be an astrophysicist, you DON'T want to be a lonely astrophysicist owing to your impoverished experience with the human race.)

2. Set Goals

Learn to set specific goals and have a plan by which to achieve them.

José Galvez balanced his schoolwork with a part-time job as a copyboy for his local paper and set concrete goals for himself. After eight years with his hometown paper, José became a photojournalist for the *Los Angeles Times*.

"Get as much out of the smaller places as you can," José advises, "then run with it from there. Shoot for the stars."

3. Be Decisive

A wrong decision is better than no decision at all. If you spend a year as a pre-med student, loathe it and then switch to French, you haven't wasted a year. You've learned something valuable—what you like and what you don't, or, put another way, what you'd be good at and what you'd be not so good at. And you've acted accordingly. Bravo for self-assertion.

Sandra Day O'Connor, the Supreme Court Justice, learned about decision making early in her career as a trial judge.

"I put all the time and effort in at the front end, trying to decide a case correctly in the first place and, doing best I can. Then I don't look back and I don't agonize over it. I may have to live with the consequences, but I'm going to live with them without regrets, because I made the best decision I could at the time."

Learn to analyze your options and then make your move quickly. Don't dilly-dally in thermodynamics if Neo-Impressionism is what you love. Decisiveness goes a long way toward the glorious destiny.

4. Believe in Yourself

Know that you can succeed. The only difference between You and Them is that you've got the motivation to get the job done.

Jim Cochran developed self-confidence while attending the University of California, Davis. He had a part-time job for three years as a basketball referee for the intramural sports program. During his third year he was the head student official.

"When making a call, it's all in the manner in which you carry yourself. If you blow the whistle and hesitate, wringing your hands, gnashing your teeth, people may pick up on your indecision. The fans and players will jump all over you, grabbing you by the collar and chanting, 'Blood! Blood! Blood!' "

Gordon Bock, a Columbia graduate, was working as a reporter for UPI when he heard that a *U.S. News & World Report* editor was coming to town. In a "Jobs" file Gordon had kept a newsletter from four years earlier that quoted the editor as saying he would hire as many journalism school students as he could. Gordon sent a letter to the editor reminding him of this promise, adding, "I'm volunteering to help you in this lofty goal."

The editor hired Gordon. "I think he was impressed that I took that statement and threw it back at him, instead of begging for a job," Gordon says.

5. Go for It

Lauren Ward, a brand marketing manager with Pepsi in Purchase, New York, says getting a job as resident assistant her junior year was one of the most valuable "business lessons" she learned during college.

When Lauren applied for her job at the end of her sophomore year, she was refused an application for a resident assistant position because she had never lived in a dorm before. Since Lauren had transferred her sophomore year from Gettysburg College in Pennsylvania, it was impossible for her to gain admission to the wait-listed dorms. Still, the interviewing board would make no exception. There were too many people applying for the RA positions. Rules are rules.

Lauren was determined to get a fair shot. She went up the hierarchy to the Director of Housing to ask for some rule bending so that she could be considered with other applicants. She listed all of her qualifications, showed her keen interest and enthusiasm for the dorms and the women who lived there and diplomatically presented her case. The Director of Housing allowed her to be interviewed.

Out of forty-four applicants, Lauren was the only one to score a perfect 10 with each of the six interviewers. She was accepted as an RA.

The business lesson? As Lauren succinctly put it, "no" does not necessarily mean "no." People will always resist change—in school, in business, at home. Count on it. Action takers don't take "no" for an answer; they can't if they want to get anything done. If you believe in something, whether it be yourself, your product, your ideas or somebody else's, be prepared to utilize creative alternatives to combat the stonewalling you'll find yourself up against time and time again.

Lauren, like Jim, believed in herself and convinced others of her abilities. If she hadn't been 100 percent confident when she had her appointment with the Director of Housing, she would have been cooked. But once she had the interview, she had no problem convincing the panel of interviewers that she had potential.

Now it's your turn. Take the ball and start running. Stockholm is only 6,347 miles from Duluth. *Adiós.*

·4·

TAKE THE PLUNGE
Managing Your Time
and Study Habits

Education has really only one basic factor . . . one must want it.
G. E. WOODBURY

The direction in which education starts a person determines his or her future life.
PLATO

While writing this book, I gave a few seminars in the New York area to seniors in high school preparing for success in college. At the beginning of each seminar, I distributed a questionnaire to get the students thinking about what really scared, bothered, excited or disgusted them when they thought about college. The opener was "What do you fear most about starting college?" Here are the responses from students in one seminar:

1. "I fear failing my freshman year."
2. "I fear the extra work that I will actually have to do."
3. "I fear loneliness, being stuck at a college that I hate and failing."
4. "I fear studying all day and night."
5. "I fear that college will be a letdown from what I've imagined."
6. "I fear not having a good time."
7. "I fear the work."
8. "I fear getting lost."
9. "I fear the work."
10. "I fear making friends and finding my classes."
11. "I fear all the work and making new friends."
12. "I fear too much pressure."

13. "I fear not doing well academically."
14. "I fear the work."
15. "I fear not fitting in."
16. "I fear that I will become so socially active that I will not pay attention to my classes."
17. "I fear not being able to compete, work and do well."
18. "I fear the responsibility and the work load."
19. "I fear I will not be able to support myself through school."
20. "I fear not finding a date."
21. "I fear I won't like my roommates. I'm afraid of leaving home and meeting new friends."
22. "I fear being on my own."
23. "I fear that I won't have a good time."
24. "I fear that I won't succeed."
25. "I fear the academic load."
26. "I fear not 'getting something' from my education."
27. "I fear that I will oversleep."
28. "I fear not doing well in class, having problems with roommates and running out of money."
29. "I fear not being able to complete, understand or do well on tests."
30. "I fear academic difficulties and no free time."
31. "I fear the work."
32. "I fear the work."
33. "I fear the work."

Notice any pattern? Almost everyone is nervous about starting college. That's understandable. It's a big step. But it's like the first day of school in first grade. It only seems like a big deal until the second day, after which you know what to expect.

The key is to convert your fears into positive actions which will help you conquer your academic weaknesses and master the skills needed for success in college.

"I never studied in high school," says Jon Jannes, a former high school basketball star who is now an education major at Northern Illinois University. "It took me two years of college to learn to study effectively." Jon spent those first two years at Black Hawk Community College.

Unlike Jon, Matt Jacobson was a top student at Alleman Catholic High School. He was on the honor roll and was captain of the football team and class valedictorian.

"I didn't study much in high school—I just made sure I was ahead of everyone else," says Matt, now a pre-law freshman at Northwestern University. "But college was a lot different. I was so overwhelmed and excited about being away from home for the first time that I didn't study much my first semester. As a result, I didn't do very well. Since I'm on scholarship, I'll have to do better next semester." One of the challenges Matt faces is improving his grades while honoring his extracurricular commitments—as a fraternity pledge, a member of the pre-law association and an assistant at the campus library.

Succeeding scholastically in college is very similar to succeeding in every other area of your life: first make an honest self-appraisal of your strengths and weaknesses, then develop a game plan to achieve your goals.

Your Major

Some college students know from day one that they want to major in chemistry to become doctors, or major in business or a particular field of engineering. For these students, there is generally a set curriculum defined by the college with some latitude for elective courses.

However, if you are like many college freshmen, and you haven't decided on a major, you may want to stick to a broad, general curriculum for your first year until you can narrow down your true interests. (I didn't declare a major until the end of my sophomore year.)

Employers often urge students who are undecided on a major to gain a broad liberal arts or business education.

"I believe that businesses should go back to basics in recruiting, should forget about the business schools and recruit the best young liberal arts students we can find," says Felix Rohatyn, a senior partner at one of New York's largest investment firms.

Other recruiters suggest more of a balance.

A recent survey conducted by Dr. Michael Useem of Boston University notes that many companies will pay for young managers with liberal arts degrees to work for MBAs, while few companies will pay for managers who majored in business to work for master's degrees in liberal arts.

Whatever you choose as a major, keep your mind open and seek knowledge outside of your own area of study.

The First-Year Schedule: Some Ideas

Here are some samples of some general curricula which will serve you well in any major you select:

First Semester	Units	Second Semester	Units
Sample A:			
Freshman Composition	3	Freshman Composition	3
Algebra (or Calculus)	3	American Government	3
Introduction to Psychology	3	Astronomy	4
French I	4	French II	4
Economics	3	Art History	3
Total	16		17
Sample B:			
Freshman Composition	3	Freshman Composition	3
Biology	4	Calculus	3
American History	3	Music Appreciation	3
Spanish I	4	Spanish II	4
Racquetball	1	Anthropology	3
Total	15		16

Consult your school catalogue or counselor for more information on courses and majors.

General advice: Take fewer, not more, courses your first semester. You'll have many adjustments to make, so it's better to be underworked than to be overextended. If you take fifteen or sixteen units you'll be in good shape.

A good scholastic start should be your first concern. The knowledge you gain in college and the grades you earn don't assure job success but will make you more attractive to a prospective employer. Good students are organized and responsible. Top marks show you're able to learn and are willing to work. Aside from helping you get a job, a sound education will open all kinds of other doors for you. An educated mind is your most valuable asset.

The Professor's Point of View

Frank Landy, an industrial organizational psychologist at Penn State, teaches introductory psychology on a regular basis. "My first class each semester is on study tips," says Landy. He discusses different methods for learning, taking notes and preparing for various exams. "If students learn basic habits of discipline and time management early, they will do best over the long haul," says Landy.

"I plunge into the material at the beginning of the semester, so I expect students to know what they're doing," says Doug Finnimore, who teaches the calculus-based physics course for engineers at Iowa State. Finnimore expects students to hit the ground running once he starts class, but if they need help, he encourages them to seek out him or any of the teaching assistants who lead the discussion sections. "The people who do well in my course come to class and work throughout the semester, while the ones who do poorly show up once in a while."

If you're not a great student, don't be overwhelmed by past failure. There are certain tips that work well for all kinds of people—those who are common-sense smart, those who have high IQs and those who may be infinitely wise. Consider the skills which all good students have, regardless of their particular learning aptitude:

1. Managing time
2. Prioritizing what has to be done
3. Taking notes
4. Studying and taking tests effectively

Managing Time

Time is money, so why not budget it? Even a billionaire's calendar has just twelve months.

As a student, you have many different classes, and if you're going to engage in extracurricular activities or part-time work, you're going to have to make a time budget and then stick to it. There's no other way. It doesn't have to be elaborate. Consider Benjamin Franklin's typical schedule:

5 a.m.	Wake up, wash and dress; plan the day; breakfast
8 a.m.	Work
12 noon	Lunch; read
2 p.m.	Work
6 p.m.	Relax; dine; review the day
10 p.m.	Sleep

It's simple enough, and yet this daily schedule served him well for over sixty years. (I'm not sure what he did for three hours each morning before he started work, but . . . !)

In his autobiography, Lee Iacocca writes, "The ability to concentrate and use your time wisely is everything if you want to succeed in business—or almost anywhere else for that matter." As an engineering major at Lehigh University, Iacocca had to balance his studies, his job on the school newspaper and his other extracurricular activities. "You've got to know what's important and then give it all you've got," says Iacocca. "Anyone who wants to become a problem solver in business has to learn fairly early how to establish priorities."

Why is writing down your schedule so important? For one thing, writing things down commits you to action. Second, it helps you determine which things are most important. The "do or die" things you have to do each day take priority over things you should do if you can find time. Third, crossing things off your list gives you a sense of accomplishment. Your schedule enables you to be in control.

Following are some sample schedules from college freshmen. (Something less perfect will do as well.)

Sample Schedule #1

MONDAY

6:30	Wake up, breakfast
7:15	Read history assignment, Chapter 3
9	Calculus
10	Freshman composition
11	Astronomy
12	Lunch
1	Library time
1–2	Calculus homework
2–3	Finish rough draft of paper on *A Farewell to Arms*
3–4	Read Chapter 4 in astronomy, review and highlight class notes
4	See composition instructor, review rough draft, make notes for revision
5	Golf class
6:30	Dinner

TO DO TODAY

1. Buy Madeline's birthday card
2. Bring Eric to coalition meeting
3. Finish history reading before class tomorrow
4. Double-check calculus
5. Finish draft of paper

8	Revise composition paper, double-check calculus homework
9:30	Madeline's surprise birthday party in the dorm
10:30	Sleep

Sample Schedule #2

MONDAY

8:30	Wake up
9:30	Management Information Systems
10:30	Computer Center-run program
11	Begin reading *The Odyssey*
12	Introduction to the humanities
1	Lunch
2	Accounting
3	Marketing Club meeting, bring advertising plans
4	Library
4–5	Accounting homework
5–6	French lab work
6–7	*The Odyssey*
7	Dinner at student union with Cynthia and Alex
8–9	Write rough draft for composition assignment on "Ode on a Grecian Urn"
10	Watch the news, read the paper
11	Review French for tomorrow's test
11–12	Organize/write schedule for tomorrow

TO DO TODAY

1. Finish French assignment
2. Run program
3. Begin *The Odyssey*
4. Meet with Marketing Club
5. Double-check accounting

Let's be realistic. Only the truly obsessive would have schedules this detailed. But it does help to make some kind of daily game plan.

PBF

As a college student, you will probably be able to plan your class schedule. Use that flexibility to your advantage. "I work best late at night," says Karen McMillen. "My best semesters were those where I had no taxing classes earlier than 9 or 10 a.m. I hit a slump right after lunch, so I found that giving myself two to three hours off in the middle of the day worked well. "I could focus better on my classes if they were scheduled during my 'peak brain function' times."

Learning to Think

The first step is deciding that you want to be a good student. College is more challenging than high school. Rote memorization won't cut it. You'll have to learn to think critically.

"Learning to think is the most important thing you can get out of college," says Bobbie Katz, who attended McGill University in Canada.

Bobbie, now a lawyer with Milbank, Tweed, Hadley and McCloy, a Wall Street firm, wanted to be a gym teacher when he started college. The more he found out about his future profession, however, the less well suited to it he felt he was. Ultimately he opted not to pursue physical education. But because he had a broad liberal arts education, he learned to make good use of his mind, disciplining himself to think in increasingly complex ways.

Active Learning

Become an active learner. How? Well, one way is to finish your assigned reading (or at least skim it) before you attend a lecture. That way the professor's comments become a review for you—not an introduction.

But don't think you can do the reading and skip the class. That's what Jason Moore tried to do his first semester at the University of Washington. What he discovered —much to his dismay—was that some of the material covered on exams came from lectures.

If your professor's lectures are supplemented by discussion groups led by graduate teaching assistants, attend them. Ask questions. Assert yourself.

Taking Effective Notes

Frank Landy, the professor from Penn State, found the notebook of one of his students. "Since I had just given what I thought was a particularly clear, well-delivered lecture, I opened the book to see what kind of notes the student took. To my dismay and surprise, the student had written down only the anecdotes and stories which described the main points. The real meat of the lecture was scribbled in the margins as an afterthought."

Professors will often use stories or real-life applications to explain a concept or term. "The bones," says Landy, "are the theory, while the flesh is the story." To truly learn the subject matter, you must listen for and grasp both.

To take good notes you must go to class. Don't kid yourself. You need the material which your professors give you in the lecture, no matter how well you've read and retained the information in the texts.

Most professors will organize their lectures around several controlling points. Obviously, you can't write everything down, but you will want to record the main ideas. Some people organize their lectures in outline form. Others write in more of a prose style which can be highlighted later on. Find a style that's comfortable for you and stick to it.

Keep your notes organized and in one place. Date each set of notes so that you can easily match the lecture with the corresponding text chapter. If necessary, go back and rewrite your notes after the lecture. Or sit down with your professor during his or her office hours and make sure you understand the information.

Review your notes in the same way that you continually review the summaries after every chapter. If you keep up with the material, studying for exams will be a whole lot easier. You can't cram for life, so start your good planning habits now. You'll be prepared for the long haul.

Get to Know Your Professors

John Diaz is a reporter for the *Denver Post*. He also serves on a PBS affiliate panel every Friday night, where he discusses issues central to the state of Colorado. Recently, John taught a news-writing course at Colorado State University.

"I was amazed at how few students sought me out," said John. "The ones who went the extra nine yards to ask me outside of class how they could improve benefited the most from the course."

John was surprised that one of his students, a journalism major, said she didn't have time to read the newspaper.

"That's like an aspiring doctor who doesn't have time to be with sick people," John says. John was able to help this student prioritize her time so that she could read the paper every day, and he helped her brainstorm other career avenues to ensure that journalism was what she truly wanted to pursue. John was both a teacher and a mentor to her.

Few college students bother to get to know their professors. They don't visit during office hours unless they fail a test or miss a class. Your college professors are an invaluable resource. Start to visit their offices during the first few weeks of school. Let them know that you are truly interested in learning their material. They will be impressed by your diligence and your willingness to go above and beyond what is expected. If you have a good rapport with a professor, he or she will probably give you the benefit of the doubt if your grade is on the border between an A and a B. If you are trying hard to learn the material, chances are your professors will recognize and admire your tenacity.

What about the aloof professors who would rather spend time doing research than talking with undergrads? Well, you're going to meet them. So instead of giving up and assuming that all professors are like that, go to the ones who are willing to help. And remember: you are the consumer. You are paying for your education and you deserve your professors' attention. Each semester you'll probably have at least one professor who becomes your "favorite." Pursue the aloof ones too. It will build your confidence and it will prepare you for the aloof people you will need to establish relationships with in business.

Think of these professors as "senior advisers." They can start you thinking about your major, inspire you to superior effort and give you insights on how to learn, think more broadly and achieve your goals. The best professors you have in college are similar to the best managers you will have in the working world. Learning from them will go a long way toward teaching you what being the best means—as manager or teacher.

The cynic in you may call this brownnosing. Resist the impulse. Many "brown-nosers" who work hard and build successful relations with peers and professors achieve the best grades, get the best recommendations and go on to get top jobs.

Mastering Your Writing Skills

"Look for examples of great writers so that you can have the best models for your own work," says Greg McCaslin, who has taught students from kindergarten to college. "Read the newspaper, ask your teachers to let you see the work of some of the best writers in your class and seek styles which vary from your own." Greg, who taught for fifteen years before becoming director of the New York Foundation for the Arts, says that with writing, as with learning anything else, the determination to improve and a nondefensive response to criticism will overcome any lack of aptitude.

Freshman composition may be one of the most important classes you take in college. Even if it's not required, try to take a writing class your first semester. Learning to become a good writer means learning to communicate—to refine and develop your thoughts—so that what you mean to say, or what you think, is clear to others. If you learn to write well as a freshman, writing research papers as a sophomore, junior and senior won't be as daunting.

In the business world, good writing is essential. Throughout your career, you'll be writing memos, business letters to clients, reports, strategy and planning proposals, persuasive or informative speeches and more. If you can communicate effectively on paper and in speech, you'll have an advantage over those people who know how to manipulate numbers but know little about expressing themselves or their work.

"I try to make it fun," says David Plane, who teaches geography at a large state university. He helps his students understand their audience by asking them to write from the point of view of someone in the field. "I ask them to write on a topic and pretend that they are an urban planner. What questions would that person ask? How would they best explain and communicate their ideas to a reviewing committee or to their managers?" The next week he might ask them to write a paper from the manager's point of view, presenting the urban planner's proposal.

Becoming a good writer means becoming good at revising your thoughts and observations. Writing, like thinking, is a process. Working on several drafts helps distill your ideas. So get comfortable with rewriting, crossing things out, and throwing away some of your initial thoughts. That's part of the fun of writing.

Among the many composition books available, I think *The Simon & Schuster Handbook for Writers* by Lynn Troyka stands out. It explains how to become a good—even a great—writer. It also contains everything you need to know about the rules for writing. After your freshman year, you'll use it to write your research papers for your higher-level courses.

Here's an excerpt which should help clarify how *you* (and everybody else) can master the art of writing:

> Many people assume that a real writer can pick up a pen (or sit at a typewriter or a word processor) and magically write a finished product word by perfect word. Experienced writers know better. They know that writing is a process, a series of activities that start the moment they begin thinking about a subject and end when they complete a final draft. Experienced writers know, also, that good writing is rewriting. Their drafts are filled with additions, deletions, rearrangements, and rewordings.

So remember that good writing means practicing. And be patient with yourself. You're embarking on many new things at once.

Tips for Becoming Better at Writing

1. Keep up your journal. You'll be able to look back over your entries to see if your thoughts are coherent. Do your sentences make sense? What style do you use?

2. Write letters—instead of picking up the phone to call your friends or parents. Do your thoughts flow easily? If they don't at first, don't worry. And remember that you are going to improve with practice (as well as lower your phone bill!).

3. Read newspapers and magazines. Analyze the writing of columnists and reporters. What is clear and crisp about their writing? How could you apply the same techniques?

4. Have a friend look at and comment on your writing. Your teacher is not the only resource for feedback. Meet with a friend or two outside of your composition class and do some peer editing. Analyze their writing and ask them to make constructive criticisms of your work.

5. Write your thoughts down on lists which you can refine later. Jotting things down before you have to write—or think—them out helps crystallize your original thoughts.

How to Get Help

If you find out early that you're having problems reading, writing or understanding class material, get help fast. You can hire a professional or you can go to one of the tutors your campus may provide. If you need to take off a semester to refine your study skills, do it. It will be well worth your time and energy in the long run. Better to make mediocre grades for one semester than for four years.

Christina Bernstein felt "unmotivated" during her sophomore year in college. She was especially challenged by the language requirement, which called for four semesters of a foreign language. After spending the first semester of her junior year living with a family in Bogotá, Colombia, Chris was able to return to school speaking Spanish fluently. She not only finished up her language classes but also had new enthusiasm for the rest of her studies after taking a semester off.

To help you start focusing on your study skills, fill in the academic evaluation chart below:

ACADEMIC STRENGTHS   ACADEMIC WEAKNESSES

1. _____   1. _____

2. _____   2. _____

3. _____   3. _____

If at First You Don't Succeed . . .

You may fall short of some of the goals you set for your freshman year. Maybe you won't make 3.0 or captain the freshman football team. Instead of dwelling on your defeats, think about ways to improve next year. Sharpen your study skills? Manage time better? Apply yourself to your studies above all else until you improve? Whatever your problem, see what can be done in the summer before your sophomore year begins. You may want to spend part of the summer taking reading and writing courses.

Maybe you gave it your best shot and you've come to the conclusion that you're just not cut out for college. Okay, it's not the end of the world. It does mean, however, that you'll have a somewhat different career path than the college grad.

Martin Davis, the chief executive officer of Paramount Communications, never attended a day of college. Jack Naughton never graduated from high school. He sold Fuller brushes and La-Z-Boy recliners until he had a brainstorm: a reclining chair which dentists could use more effectively to treat their patients. He patented the idea internationally and made a fortune. The original chair, by the way, is now in the Smithsonian Museum.

But unless you have the unbridled ambition and fortitude to forgo a traditional education, you're better off staying in school. You may never be on the dean's list or make Phi Beta Kappa. That's okay. The most you can do is try, learn as much as you can and go forward. Most people improve with time. The classroom is not the only proving ground.

·5·

STAND UP AND
BE COUNTED
Extracurricular Activities

Is there any way of predicting the capacity to lead? The only way I know is to look at college records. If a student was a leader during his college years, the odds are that he will emerge as a leader in middle life.

DAVID OGILVY, of Ogilvy & Mather advertising agency

"**Y**ou've got to make it happen," says John García, who believes that belonging to organizations is a great way to enjoy yourself and meet people. John, who was a civil engineering major, was hired by Sandia National Laboratories in Albuquerque, New Mexico. Sandia sent him to Purdue to get a master's degree in structural engineering.

"Engineers are typically great theoreticians and scientists," says John, "but most of them have a hard time getting their ideas across." To balance his college experience, John worked part-time, skied, hiked and was active in the engineering honorary, Tau Beta Pi.

Lynn Ewing buried herself in her books during her freshman year at Notre Dame. "That was the worst semester I ever had," says Lynn, whose grades were far below the goals she set for herself. "The next semester, I joined the choir, the school newspaper and a religious group. My grades went way up. So did my morale and the number of friends I could count on. I kept busy, managed my time and no longer felt sorry for myself for being from out of state and away from my friends and family."

Dawn Pakluda, who graduated last May, began college at the University of Texas at Austin. She wishes she had joined extracurricular activities. "I could have had a lot more fun and met many more people during college," says Dawn. "Since I only studied and worked, I feel

I don't have the strong friendships and rich experiences that college should provide."

My own college activities included a sorority, several honoraries, volunteer work at a hospice for cancer patients and the International Students Club's English tutoring program for foreign students.

Although large group projects taught me leadership skills in a broad context, the one-on-one contacts I developed through my other activities helped me to "read" people. I learned to listen, to question, to analyze problems and to motivate even the most unenthusiastic.

Join extracurricular activities to expand your world. You'll be more interesting and you'll learn to work with people. By understanding others, you'll better understand yourself. Most important, you'll have fun.

To succeed in business, you must be a "team player." Those who give beyond what's expected command the respect of their peers and supervisors, not to mention self-respect. Chances are greater they'll be promoted to management positions to motivate others. Being valuable to an organization in college will teach you how to become valuable to a company.

Companies want to hire employees who will go above and beyond what is expected of them. If you balance work, school and play, you'll be prepared to juggle your career and personal life. You'll learn to think of new ideas and projects and you'll learn to be the first person to volunteer for additional responsibility. The busiest people are often the ones who are most likely to take on new projects because they know how to manage their time.

What does the college recruiter learn about you from your extracurricular activities?

1. You are a self-starter.
2. You've got your act together enough to balance classes with activities.
3. You like people and get along with them. You can be a team player.
4. You aren't one-dimensional; you know there's a world beyond the classroom.

Sometimes extracurriculars can lead you straight into the business world. During her freshman year in college, Jeannine DeLoche became a writer for *Course Guide*, a student publication which reviews most classes at the college. After writing more articles than the rest of the staff, she was promoted to executive editor. When she needed extra money she decided to apply for a job as an editorial assistant, banking on her *Course Guide* experience. Her first interview was for *The Wall Street Journal*. "I remember the interviewer saying, 'You have real editing experience. That's unusual in someone your age.' He offered me the job right on the spot!" Jeannine continued to work as an assistant to the editorial features editor of the *Journal* while in school. She's considering staying there after graduation next May. "Try to find extracurriculars which may match your career interests. That way, you can develop the necessary skills and see if you enjoy the work," Jeannine advises.

Develop Friendships

One of the greatest reasons to join any organization is that you meet interesting people, some of whom will become your close friends (or dates or both!). Unless you're a social recluse, developing friendships in college will be central to your happiness.

Participate

In addition to collegiate and noncollegiate organizations, keep your eyes open for other groups that might intrigue you. Consult campus counseling for lists of activities. Read the school paper. Check bulletin boards. Then plunge in. Remember, the more things you go after, the more things you'll get. Once you find a group you like, participate fully. Volunteer to chair projects. Accept responsibility. Run for office. And if you don't get accepted by Kappa Psi Whatever or you get cut from the snorkeling squad, don't be discouraged. Try something else!

Become a Leader

A leader is someone who, among other things, motivates, teaches, trains and organizes others. These skills will help you in almost any career—whether you want to start your own burger business or become President of the United States. Leadership skills developed in college will keep the door of management open for you. You may never want to manage anybody. But it's nice to have the option.

Being a leader doesn't mean you have to run the country. But wherever you work there will be a circle of people you spend most of your time with. Be a leader for them.

How do you become a leader? Well, if you haven't done it before, start small. Volunteer to head a committee. Then put as much energy into it as your studies allow. The most important part of your activity is gaining the goodwill of those you work with. As your confidence increases, accept more responsibility. Run for office. If you win, great— accept it as a sign that your peers respect you. If you lose, don't be discouraged. As Winston Churchill said: "Success is the ability to go from one failure to another with no loss of enthusiasm."

What Makes a Good Participant?

1. Contributes ideas
2. Organizes events
3. Interests others
4. Volunteers
5. Follows through on commitments
6. Recognizes others' achievements and contributions

What Makes a Good Leader?

1. Has a vision of where the organization can go
2. Makes decisions
3. Motivates others
4. Sets goals
5. Plans and organizes
6. Listens carefully
7. Inspires people
8. Delegates responsibility
9. Shares credit
10. Isn't arrogant
11. Acts diplomatically

Don't worry if you've never led before. Give it a try and see how it feels. You may hate it. But you might love it. Either way, it pays to know.

Volunteer Work

There are good business reasons for volunteering. You can be both a leader and a participant when you volunteer your time to help the disadvantaged. You'll better understand people who've had fewer opportunities than you.

Several companies encourage community service as part of their philosophy. IBM has implemented numerous community service programs to help their employees balance the demands of their jobs and their personal and family lives. One such program, Community Service Assignments, allows IBM employees to continue earning their salaries while working for nonprofit organizations. CSA helps selected nonprofit community service organizations in their time of need, and at the same time supports IBM employees with special talents in their efforts to help such organizations.

Volunteer work is a great stress release because it takes you out of yourself and away from campus. Your history final will seem less daunting after you've worked an afternoon in a children's hospital ward, or played basketball with a fatherless child, or analyzed a famous painting with a group of high school students.

If you've been active in volunteer work, your future employer will realize that you care about people and the community. If you feel that volunteering is an important part of your "life philosophy," your future employer will also know that you are a good person to hire. Employers want to hire people who will be role models for others. Good citizenship is good business.

Campus Organizations

Where do you begin? There are literally hundreds of clubs on and off campus. Start small if you're not used to groups. Try one club and then another a few months later. Below are some initial suggestions. Refer to the Associations and Organizations appendix in the back of the book.

Alumni Association
Amnesty International
Association for Afro-Americans
Campus politics
Chess Club
Choir/Orchestra
Crisis Intervention Center
Dorm Association
Greeks (fraternities and sororities)
Honorary Service Societies
International Students Club
Intramural sports and recreation
Karate Club

Literary magazine
Marketing Club
Math Club
Political groups
Pre-Law Society
Real Estate Club
Red Cross Campus Representative
Religious groups
Sailing Club
Ski Club
Student Bar Association
Student media
Student newspaper
Student Union
Theater group
Women's groups
Yearbook

Academic and Professional Honoraries

Phi Beta Kappa, Tau Beta Pi, Blue Key National Honor Society, Mortar Board, Golden Key, National Honor Society, Who's Who Among American College Students

Off-Campus Organizations

League of Women Voters
Political campaigns

Volunteer Organizations

Campus hospital
Childhood Abuse Center
Drug addiction clinics
Fund drives
Homeless shelters
Hospice Program for Cancer Patients
Hospital care
March of Dimes
Mental health services
Museums
Nursing homes
Planned Parenthood
Public Library

Red Cross
Ronald McDonald House
Sierra Club
World Wildlife Foundation

To What Extent Should You Participate?

That depends on you. Steve Kendall's college grades were average because he was captain of his college tennis team. Although his rigorous training and travel left him little spare time, Steve's athletic and academic record prompted the college recruiter for Procter and Gamble to seek him out for an interview during his senior year.

"Because I was successful in a competitive sport, Procter and Gamble believed I would apply the same principles of diligence, effort, teamwork and competition to my future career," says Steve. P and G's faith was well placed. Steve worked for them for several years before accepting his current position in sales and marketing at Nabisco.

What if your forehand is anemic? Does that mean that extracurricular activities are off limits? Of course not.

Leigh Talmage was president of her sorority, a member of scholastic honoraries each year, and spent two semesters in London. "Get activities under your belt," advises Leigh. "That's what counts the most at interview time."

A foreign bank trader, Leigh is one of five women out of 250 people in the world who trade international debt. Leigh is considering another career working for a nonprofit organization. "All of the activities and leadership positions I held in college have given me solid, transferable management skills," she says. "Because of these skills, I feel comfortable moving from one industry to another."

"It's problems with people, not problems in engineering, which constitute the real power structures," says Steven Fisher, a senior engineer for Westinghouse in San Francisco. "If you swallow your ego and learn from others in your small group, you'll pick up the common-sense aspects of the job which the technical training you receive in college doesn't provide."

Steven, who graduated from Stanford with a degree in mechanical engineering, thinks extracurricular activities are the best way to learn how to get things done. "That's how you prepare yourself to be successful in the long term with a company. You must realize how people work, what motivates them, and what the company can do to help them be happy and productive."

Sports, Anyone?

Exercise—even if you hate it. Why? Because a healthy body and mind can work and play longer and better. Because you'll return to work with a renewed sense of vigor. Because sports provide you with an opportunity to meet people.

Growing up with four St. Louis Cardinal baseball-fanatic brothers, I resisted sports. I never learned to play tennis or golf and I was easily bored at football and basketball games. Although I'm still not thrilled at watching sports, I've grown to love running (a sport which requires, thank God, little talent). I still regret that I wasn't more athletically active during college. Now I would have it no other way.

Sports like tennis and golf are favorite corporate pastimes. In fact, many business deals and discussions take place on the tennis court or the golf course. Entertainment is a big part of business, and sports entertainment is no different.

What If You Don't Get Accepted into Organization X?

Does that mean you've failed? Of course not. You only fail if you don't try. It sounds trite, but it's true.

I didn't get into a lot of things I applied for in college. My freshman year, I didn't make it into the freshman honorary. I was disappointed. But before I said, "To hell with it," I stopped to think about *why* I didn't make it in. Had I blown the interview? Was I not as well rounded as other people? Were my grades not as good? Comparatively, the other people who made it were better qualified. Throughout the next year I worked on the areas which needed improvement and, at the end of the year, I applied for the sophomore honorary. I was accepted.

Another big disappointment came my junior year when I applied for the Rotary Scholarship and didn't even make the first cut. I had invested a lot of time and energy filling out the lengthy application, getting all my professors to write me letters of recommendation and fully researching the three countries in which I wanted to study. They wanted an "ambassador of goodwill," which I thought I could be! But there were others who were more qualified: I had to accept that.

It was almost as painful as when I was sixteen and didn't make cheerleading for the second year in a row. I was devastated. But the application hadn't been a waste of time. I learned how much I truly loved studying other cultures. I swore to make travel a major life priority. I met fascinating people who were also applying for the scholarship.

One of them, a person who spoke fluent Chinese, Spanish and French, became my first true love. That experience was probably more rewarding than a scholarship which would have sent me around the world! (He didn't make the first cut either. We commiserated together.)

When you get a job after college, you may initially be passed over for a promotion you want. Chances are you were not as well qualified as the person who got the job. Find out what you can do to ensure that you get the next opening, and TAKE ACTION.

Don't let defeats defeat you. If you learn in college how to graciously handle disappointments, you'll be well prepared for the working world, where you'll need to transform losses into new challenges and opportunities.

Lex Kaplan, who launched his own magazine, says, "Honorable failures are worth a lot more than easy successes, especially if the successes occur in a field that doesn't interest you."

Dealing with Your Supporters . . . and Detractors

Whenever you assert your opinions about what you think an organization should or shouldn't do, some people will agree with you and others won't. Sometimes, especially if you are leading an organization, you will have to stick your neck out for what you believe in.

Be cool. If people always agreed with you, life would be dull. The best ideas and the best teamwork come from stimulating discussions which allow all points of view to be considered. But when people disagree with you—and sometimes during college and in the real world they will disagree violently—keep a positive attitude and remain confident. Acknowledge their opposing viewpoints and thank them for their suggestions. Remaining mature and controlled helps you to put the situation into perspective and allows you to reaffirm your position. Remember, leaders are sometimes unpopular. That's okay. It's helpful to get used to this feeling in college—to let your skin get thicker—so that you will be more resilient dealing with people of varying maturity levels once you start working.

Part of being a leader and a participant is learning how to elicit the best suggestions and ideas from others. Discussing your thoughts with your colleagues often helps you to improve a good idea of your own. Recognize that it's good to change your mind sometimes, to concede to someone else's points or plans. This is all part of developing your judgment.

·6·

THE REAL WORLD
Working Part-Time

I don't like work—no one does—but I like what is in work—the chance to find yourself. Your own reality—not for others—what no other person can ever know.

JOSEPH CONRAD, *Heart of Darkness*

The summer after his freshman year at the University of Wisconsin, Jeff Colquhoun worked at the Kellogg factory near his parents' home in Michigan. Occupation? Well, what does one do at a cereal factory? Eat and run?

Guess again. Jeff frosted flakes. And when finished with his frosting duties, he stuffed coupons by hand into boxes the machines had missed. His was a manual counteroffensive to mechanical incompetence. It was an incredibly boring job. But for Jeff it was by no means a waste of time.

Besides earning money to help pay tuition, Jeff learned several things that helped clarify his career direction.

1. The Kellogg experience opened Jeff's eyes to people whose background differed from his. There were many people there who hadn't had Jeff's advantages whom he might never have encountered in his "ordinary" college experience or in a more typical summer internship for the up-and-coming collegiate. The job helped Jeff to appreciate his education. He developed real respect for people from all walks of life who worked hard for a living, regardless of job title.

2. He did not let the "boring" aspects of the job interfere with his work or his attitude. For the purposes of sanity he stretched his

85

mind and imagination. He went through the letters of the Greek alphabet forward and backward. He marveled at the mind of the engineer who designed the machine. (He thanked God for him, in fact.)

3. Jeff learned that when you're not in an ideal situation (we seldom are), you've got to expand your mind and envision a broader context. Idle is bust.

Thirteen years later Jeff is a doctor of ophthalmology in New York City. He went through years of studying and rigorous on-the-job training in emergency settings and operating rooms. What he learned at the Kellogg factory that summer in college—to see even the most difficult or mundane tasks in a broader context—helped him pursue medicine.

Joy Wake, a marketing planner at Hallmark in Kansas City, Montana, had several part-time jobs during college. As the youngest of nine children, Joy supported herself 100 percent through college. She had several work-study jobs and one summer internship in Washington. And she saved enough money to travel one semester through Europe.

"Hallmark hired me because I had worked hard to put myself through college," Joy says. "They believed in me because I had a successful track record. They knew I could overcome obstacles. They also recognized that I had done different things to make myself stand out."

Instead of attending school during the day and working at night, Chris Barnett did the opposite. He got an entry-level job paying $185 a week selling space in the yellow pages. He took three classes at night per semester. Although it took Chris two additional years to graduate from college after transferring from the University of Southern California to Columbia, he feels the trade-off—financial and experiential—was worth it.

Chris is graduating this spring. He has been promoted three times within the last two years and is now supervising eleven people. It's true that Chris hasn't had time to join extracurricular activities or participate in intramural sports, but he has, at age twenty-four, earned a living, put himself through school and maintained a 3.2 grade point average at an Ivy League school. He's learned firsthand about leadership through direct professional experience.

Gaining work experience in college is one of the best ways to prepare for your future. First, you learn to support yourself, partially or entirely, which tells your future employer that you have a sense of commitment, responsibility and financial savvy. Second—and more important—you acquire skills and techniques that will prepare you to work with others.

What Work Is Best for You?

Almost any job you have during college will benefit you in ways far greater than the financial. Obviously, some jobs are better than others. Before you take the first job you apply for, spend some time learning about yourself and the kinds of jobs available on and off campus.

Phoebe Finn applied to several expensive acting schools in New York and London while studying drama at the University of Maryland. To support herself and save money, she drove the campus shuttle bus at night. Not glamorous for someone aspiring to be Meryl Streep. But the job served its purpose. It allowed her to save money and attend the London School of Dramatics. Phoebe's London experience helped her land her first big job in the Folger Shakespeare production of *Macbeth*.

Of course, if you've got your sights set on a highly competitive field, it may be worth it to take the extra steps necessary to get a job providing experience that will help you later on.

"Broadcasting is fiercely competitive," says Nancy Kilroy. To prepare herself during college at Yale, Nancy worked at National Public Radio, where she learned how to interview people, how to be persistent and how to pull together information for a five-minute broadcast. "Experience is everything in broadcasting," says Nancy. "You'd better learn early on that most people have already worked at least two jobs in the profession by the time they graduate."

What to Consider

As discussed in Chapter 3, there are three basic areas of work: working with people, information or objects. You might enjoy each of these areas, but if you're like most people, one appeals to you more than the other two.

Richard Bolles, the author of *What Color Is Your Parachute?*, identifies several characteristics that can help you analyze what area best suits you. How do you answer the following questions?

People-Related Skills

Taking Instruction

Do you like to take instruction and then carry out a plan?

Do you enjoy executing and providing support services?

Serving

Do you like helping, teaching, waiting on or serving others?

Sensing, Feeling

Are you intuitive with respect to the needs of others?

Are you generally responsive, empathic, warm and able to understand the position of others?

Communicating

Are you a good listener? Do you question others?

Do you enjoy writing, giving speeches, giving instructions to others?

Persuading

Do you like to influence, inspire and recruit others?

Do you like publicizing and promoting causes, people or things?

Performing, Amusing

Do you like to entertain others?

Do you like to dramatize your point of view or your own experiences as a means of teaching others?

Managing, Supervising

Do you like to plan, oversee and develop programs with people?

Do you like to encourage and critically evaluate others, using your expertise to help them to improve?

Negotiating, Decision Making

Do you like to discuss, confer and resolve difficult issues?

Are you skilled in conflict management?

Do you appreciate and consider opposing points of view?

Founding, Leading

Are you able to work with little or no supervision?

Do you have maverick qualities? That is, do you like to forge your own, possibly better path?

Can you enlist the enthusiasm and the support of others?

Do you delegate authority? Do you trust others to execute a job?

Advising, Consulting

Do you enjoy helping others resolve a physical, emotional or spiritual problem?

Do you enjoy being an expert, reading and keeping up with what is happening in one field?

Do you make effective use of contacts? Do you give others insight and perspective on their problems?

Holistic Counseling

Do you like to facilitate the growth of others by helping them to identify solutions to their problems?

Training

Do you like to teach others through lecture, demonstration or practice?

Information-Related Skills

Observing

Do you like to study the behavior of people, information or things?

Comparing

Do you enjoy analyzing two or more different things?

Copying, Storing and Retrieving

Do you like keeping records, storing data, memorizing, filing or reviewing information?

Computing

Do you enjoy working with numbers, taking inventory, solving statistical problems, using a computer, budgeting, projecting or processing data?

Researching

Do you like uncovering hard-to-find facts and information?

Analyzing

Do you like to break things down, take information apart and examine it?

Organizing

Does giving structure and order to things turn you on? Do you always have a place for everything? Do you typically classify material?

Evaluating

Are you a diagnoser or inspector? Do you like to assess, decide, appraise and summarize information or situations?

Visualizing

Are you able to perceive patterns and images? Do you picture things you want to do before you do them? Do you enjoy painting, drawing or designing?

Improving, Adapting

Do you like to take what others have developed and expand upon it? Are you good at improvising, improving and arranging?

Creating, Synthesizing

Do you like to pull together seemingly unrelated things? Do you like to develop new concepts, approaches and interpretations?

Designing

Do you like to create models, sculpture or other things?

Planning, Developing

Do you tend to oversee and carry out a plan? Do you prioritize and develop strategies?

Expediting

Do you naturally tend to speed up a task by organizing your objectives ahead of time? Do you have a sense of urgency or immediacy?

Achieving

Do you enjoy accomplishing tasks or specific goals? Do you like to increase productivity and create results?

Object-Related Skills

Manipulating

Do you enjoy working with your hands? Or do you like using your body to move objects?

Working with the Earth and Nature

Do you like nurturing, weeding, harvesting?

Feeding, Emptying (Machines)

Do you like placing, stacking, dumping and removing things from machines?

Monitoring (Machines)

Do you like monitoring and adjusting machines, pushing buttons, flipping switches, adjusting controls?

Using Tools

Do you enjoy using hand tools?

Operating Equipment or Machines

Do you like to have specialized knowledge about equipment or machines?

Operating Vehicles

Do you like to drive, pilot or steer vehicles?

Precision Working

Do you like jobs such as keypunching, drilling, sandblasting, making miniatures or performing other specialized tasks with your hands?

Setting Up

Do you like to construct or set up displays, machinery or equipment?

Repairing

Do you like to restore, repair or do preventive maintenance?

As a freshman, you may not be able to complete this questionnaire. But as a junior or senior, you'll have many more experiences under your belt. For now, just get a general idea of your strongest suit.

Below is a list of job possibilities.

Common Jobs for College Students

CAMPUS:

PEOPLE	INFORMATION	OBJECTS
Resident assistant	Word processor	Library aide
Campus guide	Administrative	Lab technician
Health aide	assistant	Mechanic
Study tutor	Secretarial aide	Maintenance
Lecturer	Writer (yearbook	assistant
	or campus	Groundskeeper
	newspaper)	
	Researcher	

COMMUNITY:

PEOPLE	INFORMATION	OBJECTS
Waiter/Waitress	Legal assistant	Short-order cook
Sales clerk	Secretary	Gas-station attendant
Host/hostess	Word processor	Technician
Bartender		Gardener/yard work

If Waiting on Tables Is Not for You . . .

If you decide to forgo a traditional part-time job, such as waiting on tables, for a more educational, experience-earning job, such as working as a legal clerk, you'll have to demonstrate to your potential employer that you are worth hiring despite your limited experience. If you can convince the person interviewing you that you are a quick learner, extremely reliable, motivated above and beyond what is expected and truly interested in pursuing a career in that area, chances are you'll get the job despite your youth and inexperience.

Remember that the people interviewing you were once in your place. A determined and inquisitive mind and the capacity to work hard and achieve enabled them to be where they are today. If your potential employer believes you have the same qualities that contributed to his success, it is in his best interest to hire you. After all, you will be graduating in a few years and you could be an attractive employee. Ask for the chance to prove what you can do. Both you and the employer could have a lot to gain.

If you don't get the experience-earning job you sought, don't despair. Follow up your interviews with a thank-you letter and reconfirm your interest in the company. If you try again six months or a year later, the company may be in a better position to take you on as an apprentice. If you know that the experience gained on the job would be more valuable than the wages you would earn and you can afford it, volunteer for the first six months. It might pay off in the long run.

The experience that a "real life" job will provide could make the difference when you are competing for the job you most want your last semester of college. If you have the solid job experience, you will most probably get hired, even if the other candidate has superior grades and a more impressive background. You learned firsthand about the job and consequently you have much more to offer than someone without such experience.

Whatever the part-time job you hold—be it gas-station attendant, hotel clerk or real estate apprentice—you'll learn to juggle work, school and other activities while sustaining your motivation and sense of self-reliance. You'll have the best-rounded education upon graduation; you'll gain satisfaction from knowing that you are self-reliant, independent and responsible for your own accomplishments; and you'll gather important data to help you make your career decisions in your junior and senior years.

·7·

INTERN WE TRUST
Getting the Internship

What we learn to do, we learn by doing.
THOMAS JEFFERSON

"**S**ummer activity is a great indicator of future job success," says Dee Milligan, first vice president and director of insurance marketing for Kemper Financial Company in Chicago, who interviews and hires many graduates straight from college. "I want to see that the applicant has taken initiative. I'm not interested in someone who has just messed around and not thought about using their summers wisely."

Dee says that working during the summer in a standard corporate environment gives students the opportunity to learn about business—by diving in and experiencing it for themselves. It's the kind of education you can't get in school.

Summer internships can be a prism through which you learn about a profession and decide if you want it as your career. If you do, the internship gives you credibility in the job market and a leg up on those with no experience. If not, you will have invested only your summer, not your life.

And remember, the company will be checking you out, too. Rita Rather is a management information systems senior at the University of Illinois. An honor student with a strong personality, she so impressed management at the Cellular Telephone Company in Chicago during her internship last summer that they offered her a full-time job upon her graduation this spring.

Internships During School

Jim Cochran is from Los Alamos, New Mexico. An economics major, he had three internships during college. He learned something different in each job.

During his sophomore year, Jim had an unpaid internship twelve hours a week with a commercial real estate company, Kimmel Property Management. This was Jim's first exposure to business and it enabled him to build confidence and establish valuable contacts. Four years later, when Jim began his first job out of college, he interviewed the president of Kimmel to ask advice on his future career. Today, Jim is still in contact with several people from his first internship.

The second internship was in the law firm of Thomas Frankel, where Jim worked ten hours a week during the school year. Jim learned here that he did not want to become a lawyer. He still did not know what he really wanted to do, but at least, by the process of elimination, he was learning what he did *not* want to do.

During his senior year, Jim worked ten hours a week for Merrill Lynch. He wanted to explore finance and investing and to continue making contacts. He enjoyed the job at Merrill, but didn't feel passionate enough about it to make it a career. He opted not to pursue a career in investing and got his first job with a real estate consulting firm.

When you know what you want to do, it can be valuable to let one internship lead to another in the same field of interest. This shows future employers you are not only interested in them—you are *very* interested in them. Gordon Bock, a former reporter with both *U.S. News & World Report* and *Time*, was the youngest news director ever at Columbia University's radio station his sophomore year. One day the nationally syndicated Campus Radio Voice called for an intern. Gordon said, "I'm interested." He was hired, and over the next two years he was heard over the air at 460 colleges nationwide, interviewing celebrities and newsmakers. That internship led to the most prestigious one of all: becoming the first undergraduate in the history of the school to teach at Columbia's Graduate School of Journalism.

The result: when Gordon graduated he moved immediately to a reporting job with AP Dow Jones in New York, writing radio copy. Three months later he was hired by UPI New York, at a third-year scale (based largely on his college jobs). And four years after that he was hired by *U.S. News & World Report*. At age twenty-six, when many reporters are moving from one-town to three-town beats, Gordon was given a job covering eight states and half of Pennsylvania at a major national magazine.

Landing good internships, Gordon says, can be very important. And once you have them, he says, make the most of them. "Be gung-ho about whatever you do."

Summer Internships

Brenda White is from Ainsworth, Iowa, a town of five hundred people. She attended Augustana, a small Lutheran college in Illinois. During her junior year, Brenda applied for a nonpaying summer internship with the United Nations. She was selected as one of twenty college students in the country to come to New York.

Although the internship was nonpaying, Brenda talked to several people at the financial aid office at Augustana to see if she could get funding. And she did. She was the only UN intern who was paid that summer.

The most valuable part of Brenda's experience? She became "street smart." She learned to survive—and thrive—in a big city. After that summer in New York, Brenda felt herself a match for any environment.

Jeff Cantany is an economics major who hopes to work for a nonprofit agency in international development. To qualify he needs to go into the Peace Corps, and they require construction skills. So what did he do the summer after his freshman year? He worked for a builder in New Mexico. He earned a good salary, learned a trade and was introduced to a culture very different from that of his native New York.

A Personal Note

I was a summer intern in Washington between my sophomore and junior years. I worked without pay for Common Cause, a grass-roots lobbying organization. I attended Senate and House hearings and reported on the Clean Air Act and the daily debate on the constitutional amendment to balance the budget.

My second internship was with Arizona senator Dennis DeConcini. It gave me a different perspective on the political process. I felt largely uninspired by politics and decided not to pursue a law degree after graduation.

Still, that summer I met many fascinating people. Because one of my brother's friends worked for Vice President George Bush, I got to attend a special reception for Prime Minister Indira Gandhi of India, which President Reagan held in the White House Rose Garden. Although I had never taken a political science course, I learned firsthand about our political process. I saw it with my own eyes.

On the less glamorous side, these internships didn't pay the bills. I had to work as a waitress—the only female worker (except for the hostess) at an Italian restaurant atop an apartment building overlooking the Washington monuments. Because the restaurant was expensive, I made good money in tips while working only three nights a week. I remember working on the Fourth of July and feeling glum because all my friends were down on the Mall watching the fireworks and listening to the Beach Boys concert. But I was lucky to be in Washington. I was also lucky to have a part-time job which enabled me to have my non-paying, though thoroughly rewarding summer internships.

Winter Internships

Many companies and firms have programs for students during the winter semester break. During his senior year at Columbia, Tim Dalton had a full-time four-week internship during January with the Lawyers Committee for Human Rights in New York City. Tim worked with other volunteers on LCHR reports on human rights violations and refugee issues.

"I learned about issues not covered in the newspapers," says Tim. "Although I wasn't paid, the internship was invaluable because I gained insight into the nonprofit organizations which rely heavily on volunteers. I provided them with much-needed labor, but most of all, I enjoyed the work."

Internships After Graduation

Think about internships after college. Kim Caldwell already had a BA in art history when she began her six-month internship at the Metropolitan Museum of Art in New York. Kim was able to work in several administrative areas of the museum and to visit other museums in the city. She got the job through Aniso, a monthly job posting put out by the American Association of Museums.

"Becoming involved in a professional organization kept me abreast of openings in the museum field as well as informing me of the latest trends in museum policies," Kim said.

No Pay? Okay

Rod García, admissions recruiter for the MBA program at the University of Chicago, says that internships are very useful for people who don't yet know what they want to do. "Internships give students an idea of what's out there. The experience that even an unpaid internship provides is just as valuable as, if not more valuable than, some of your key college courses."

Mentors

Lisa Heinlein, a special education teacher, learned a great deal about how to be an excellent teacher from watching other great teachers. "Allow yourself to be taught," Lisa says. "Don't be afraid to try things and make mistakes—that's how you learn."

During his sophomore year, Lenny Feder, now a senior at Columbia, had his first internship. He worked for three weeks at American Marketing. Though he'd held a lot of different jobs, this was his first experience in the corporate world. His boss, who happened to belong to the same fraternity as Lenny when he attended college, served as a mentor. He let Lenny sit in on meetings, allowed him to help plan projects from day one and even gave him advice on what types of suits to wear. "My mentor gave me a sense of what skills I'd need in the business world. But I couldn't just copy him. I learned those skills by myself—with my mentor serving as a guide."

Through your internships, you'll meet people who can be your teachers. Choose two or three people at work you respect to be your mentors. Pick their brains to find answers to the following questions:

1. How could you do your job better?
2. What could you do at school to better prepare yourself for this industry?
3. How did your mentors become interested in this business?
4. What are their toughest challenges?
5. What part of the job do they like most?
6. What is the toughest challenge facing the industry in the next five years?
7. Where is the growth potential?
8. If they had to hire you today, would you get the job? If not, why not?
9. Whom do they consider a qualified applicant?

Learn all you can about the job. You'll gain insight and your employers will develop respect for your enthusiasm.

When Things Go Wrong

What happens when you make your first mistakes on the job? Well, if you're not making any mistakes, you're probably not trying hard enough. Mistakes are the process by which we learn. One of the main purposes of internships is to learn some lessons that will make you better prepared once you start your "real" job after college.

Jim Burke, the CEO at Johnson & Johnson, has a favorite story about his former boss: General Robert Wood Johnson discovered that Burke had failed miserably at one of his really innovative ideas—a children's chest rub. Johnson asked him, "Are you the person who cost us all that money?" Burke nodded. "I'd like to congratulate you," the general said. "If you are making mistakes, that means you are making decisions and taking risks. And we won't grow unless you take risks."

If you mess up on the job, admit it, correct it, discuss it and, above all, learn from it. The greatest fool is one who will not admit his own mistakes or get help from others when necessary.

How to Get the Internship

Securing a summer internship is very much like interviewing for your "real" job at the end of your senior year. In fact, the whole process of writing your résumé, interviewing and landing the summer job is the best preparation for your full-fledged job search. Here's what to do:

1. Buy a copy of one of the current summer internship directories for college students, or make an appointment in your school's summer internship office. I recommend Betsy Baur's *Getting Work Experience*. (See also Appendix 2 at the back of this book.)
2. Make a list of the positions that interest you.
3. Narrow your scope by choosing the five internships you'd like best.

For example:
Desired career: personnel executive
Summer internship list:

1.

2.

3.

4.

5.

Review the list carefully. Consider what you could offer the potential employer. Where and how do you work best? Are you a self-starter or do you like to be supervised? Would you prefer a large corporation or a smaller company?

Which job will best develop your skills? Using the column on the right, fill in the column on the left. If you wish, add your own words to describe your strengths and weaknesses.

My greatest strengths:

_____   organizing

_____   working with people

_____   developing ideas

_____   writing/researching

_____   prioritizing time

_____   solving problems

_____   working with numbers

_____   observing

_____   repairing

_____   founding/leading

_____   attention to detail

_____ taking instructions

_____ speaking in public

Where?

In which region would you like to work? If you're interested in banking, New York, Chicago, Los Angeles or San Francisco would be a great city to work in for a summer. If you're interested in computers, you could work in almost any large city, though California's Silicon Valley might be the best. Maybe you don't know which career interests you yet. No problem. Half your classmates don't know either. But they're not taking steps to find out. Pat yourself on the back. Okay, that's enough. Now back to work . . .

If you can afford it, seek contrast. If you're from a small town, apply to a big city. The more diversity you experience, the more versatile you'll be. Working in new cities conveys maturity, confidence and determination to your future employers. I waited tables on the weekends so I could afford to intern a summer in New York. I'm from Arizona, and living three months in Manhattan was as educational as the job I had there.

What to Do

First, realize that you will get a job. Banish all doubts—they ain't gonna help you. So accept that you're going to succeed—okay? (If you don't think you'll succeed, why read this book?)

Now, for the practical steps: begin early. If you want to get an internship between your sophomore and junior years, you should have your résumé, cover letter and target companies ready the summer after your freshman year. Send letters to at least twenty companies and expect to receive at least two offers.

Here's what to send:

A one-page COVER LETTER stating your interests, abilities and reasons for choosing this company. This letter, like your résumé, should be flawlessly written and typed. See the example on page 142. Have a couple of your friends or your composition professor read it for clarity and accuracy. Make sure your letter is sent to the right person. Don't rely on a list. It's a changing world, so call the company.

Your RÉSUMÉ should briefly explain your objectives as an intern, your education, your work experience and your extracurricular activities. List three references and notify these people that they may be contacted by your prospective employer. If possible, ask a professor or employer (NOT one of your three references) to write you a letter of recommendation to enclose with your résumé and cover letter.

About three weeks after you've mailed your cover letter, résumé and letter of recommendation, call the person to whom you wrote. Make sure they received your letter and ask when a decision will be made. Reiterate your interest in their company but also let them know that you have other summer job options.

Is an interview required? Then read Chapter 11.

Sample Résumé
MARY ANN VAN CAMP
6680 North Anywhere Avenue
Duluth, Minnesota 00001

PERSONAL:	College sophomore English Major, Business Minor University of Georgia Athens, Georgia
OBJECTIVE:	Summer Internship in Marketing or Sales
EMPLOYMENT:	
4/89 to present:	Adler/Adler Public Relations Agency, administrative assistant. Responsibilities include working with clients, answering mail, working with partners and routine paperwork.
3/88 to 4/89:	Hostess, Spaghetti Company Restaurant.
ACTIVITIES:	Resident Assistant, Coronado Dorm. Responsibilities include organizing dorm functions, helping students adjust to college and providing support during difficult times. Member, International Students Club. Member, Spurs, Sophomore Student Honorary, Philanthropy program.

HIGH SCHOOL HIGHLIGHTS:	President, Thespian Society. Organized actors' league, performed for charities, worked with professional actors in the community. Graduated with a 3.2 GPA. Mainstream High

Junior year representative to Girls' State.

Sample Cover Letter

6680 North Anywhere Avenue
Duluth, Minnesota 00001

September 30, 1990

Mr. Ryan Rinaldi
Pillsbury Company
Pillsbury Center
Minneapolis, MN 55402

Dear Mr. Rinaldi:

I am a sophomore majoring in English and minoring in Business at the University of Georgia. I would like to work for Pillsbury this summer as an intern in either sales or marketing.

Attached is a copy of my résumé and a letter of reference from one of my professors. As you can see from my résumé, I am committed to achieving both in and out of the classroom. An internship with Pillsbury would provide me with unparalleled "real world" experience. Because I am a dedicated, energetic and inquisitive worker, I would be a benefit to Pillsbury as an intern.

I will be calling before October 15 to arrange a phone interview, if necessary. In the meantime, if you have any questions, don't hesitate to call me at 313-888-1017.

I look forward to speaking with you soon. Thank you for your consideration.

Sincerely,

Mary Ann Van Camp

Sample Letter of Recommendation

September 25, 1990

To Whom It May Concern:

I met Mary Ann Van Camp the first semester of her freshman year. Mary Ann was enrolled in my Western Civilization course and she immediately impressed me as a top-rate student. She came to see me during office hours, asked questions about class lectures and writing assignments and followed up after tests to ensure that she had learned all pertinent information. Seldom do college students today take the extra time—especially in a survey course—to get to know their professor and to seek his or her help outside of class.

Although Mary Ann received a B for the course, her efforts were A for the quality of time she devoted to a class normally taken by sophomores. The first semester of college is a tough adjustment period for any student, but those who persevere to learn the materials, not for the letter grade, but for the sake of learning, are truly distinguished. I know Mary Ann will get more than most out of college because she tries harder.

I highly recommend Mary Ann for a summer internship at your company. Her delightful personality coupled with her intellect and desire to learn would be an asset to any company or organization.

Please feel free to contact me.

Sincerely,

Dr. Robert Timmons
Department of History
University of Georgia
Athens, Georgia 00010

Only the Beginning

In Appendix 1 at the back of this book, you'll find a directory of many businesses in the United States currently offering summer internships for college students. Although this is an excellent reference list, don't depend on it completely. If no company in your field of interest is listed, find one on your own! Some of the most rewarding summer internships will be those you research and find yourself. Use this list to land your first summer internship, but for the following summer, go for the challenge of landing the job no one else could find. Sell yourself to the company which may not have an established internship program.

If you can convince an employer to "make a position" for you, you'll be successful at selling your ideas and getting support when you enter the business world. The more you develop these "maverick" qualities, the more fearless you'll become in business. To be effective you must believe in yourself and be capable of generating enthusiasm. If you learn early to convince others to believe in you, you'll be several steps ahead of the game.

Evaluating Your Internship

Some companies have formal evaluations. If yours doesn't, be forthright in asking for an honest appraisal of your work at the conclusion of your internship. Remember, you'll only be able to improve if you can take constructive criticism from those with more experience.

The following is a list of categories by which an employee is typically evaluated. Use the checklist to rate yourself and then go over it with your manager. Ask for specific tips on how you can improve on your weak areas.

PERFORMANCE REVIEW

> Quality of work
> Quantity of work
> Problem solving
> Decision making
> Planning and organizing
> Delegating
> Self-control
> Communicating
> Teamwork
> Business savvy

OTHER CHARACTERISTICS

> Creativity
> Initiative
> Work with others

Judgment
Adaptability
Persuasiveness
Leadership
Self-confidence
Attitude
Maturity
Foresight

OVERALL EVALUATION:

Strengths:
Areas for improvement:
Employee's comments:

The Last Word

If you love your internship and decide that another summer at the same company would be valuable for your professional development, set things up for the following year. Secure greater responsibilities for the next summer. Many companies have an interest in cultivating students two summers in a row, so that they can make them a job offer upon graduation.

Or you may wish to keep your options open and work for another company the following summer—in the same industry or a completely different one.

·8·

WINDOWS ON THE WORLD
Traveling at Home or Abroad

The world is a book and those who stay at home read only one page.
ST. AUGUSTINE

For my part, I travel not to go anywhere, but to go. I travel for travel's sake. The great affair is to move.
ROBERT LOUIS STEVENSON

Hong Kong. Buenos Aires. Cairo. London. Paris. Milan. Faraway cities like these can be your first exposure to other people, cultures and languages. When you venture out of your safe, familiar environment, your world expands and so does your confidence. Traveling helps you develop adaptability. You learn to adjust quickly to any situation, group of people or environment and you begin to understand how to draw on past experiences to evaluate new ones.

Linda Montag grew up in Pittsburgh and attended Grove College in Pennsylvania. Athough her school offered only study-abroad programs, Linda knew she could distinguish herself by getting work experience in a foreign country. With the encouragement of one of her German professors, she managed to enter a work-study program in Germany for one summer and one semester in an insurance company.

"My time abroad helped me develop self-confidence more than anything else I did in college," says Linda, who is now as assistant vice president of a German commercial bank with headquarters in Frankfurt. "It was the first opportunity I had to truly assert myself and depend on myself completely to do everything—from finding my way around to learning my job to becoming proficient in a foreign language."

There are many jobs abroad. Some can be found on the bulletin boards of hostels, train stations and schools. Susan Finnemore studied one semester at York College in England. On weekends she hitchhiked with friends around Great Britain. In the hostels where she stayed, she read advertisements for "work camps." She worked in a camp on a Welsh estate, where she received wages and lodging. The camp paid for food and Susan cooked the meals.

Susan's parents are both professors, and Susan had always planned to go straight from undergraduate school to a master's program in history. Travel gave her the perspective to reconsider her options. "If I can travel through Europe," Susan thought to herself, "I can do anything." Instead of going to graduate school, Susan decided to pursue a career in publishing. She is now psychology editor in the college textbook division of Prentice-Hall.

Travel doesn't have to be foreign to be valuable. After her sophomore year at Brown University, Melissa Halverstadt spent twelve months hiking, kayaking and mountain climbing in the wilderness education program at Prescott College in Arizona. She learned to lead, cooperate, conserve and plan—survival skills in the truest sense.

Nor does your travel experience have to be structured. Bill and Jonathan Aikens spent three months bicycling in Europe. Bill spoke Spanish and French; Jonathan spoke German; both learned Italian en route. The trip was inexpensive, but the experience was rich.

Travel can also provide a very specific, very tangible skill: speaking a foreign language. And in some fields, the more exotic the language, the more marketable that skill. UPI Beijing correspondent Mark Delvecchio skipped several rungs on the journalism ladder this way. Reporters can work ten years to win coveted overseas positions—and some can wait entire lifetimes for such jobs, to no avail. Mark rose out of a town reporting job on a small Connecticut weekly to his China job in a little over four years. An energetic reporter who often worked overtime, Mark made rapid progress on the basis of hard work alone, becoming city editor of a daily after only three years in the business. However, when a job opened up on UPI's foreign desk in Washington, D.C., Mark says it was his college year abroad in China, plus his University of Connecticut master's degree in Chinese history, that made the difference. "Few American reporters speak Chinese," he says. A few months after arriving in Washington, Mark was sent to Beijing. He was twenty-eight years old.

Learning exotic foreign languages also narrows the competition for scholarships. In the spring of her first year at Columbia's School of International Affairs, Elizabeth Thompson decided she wanted to go to Egypt to brush up on her Arabic. (She had learned some Arabic while abroad in the past.) Elizabeth, a native of Detroit, who attended both Harvard undergraduate school and Columbia graduate school on full scholarship, could not afford to go on her own. When she asked an academic adviser if there were any scholarships that would send her to Egypt, he pulled a grant out of a drawer. "In Middle Eastern affairs departments," he explained, "there are sometimes more grants than students."

Elizabeth spent that summer in Egypt. Since then she has taught in Syria for a year and has been admitted to Ph.D. programs in Middle Eastern studies at both Columbia and Berkeley.

When to Go

If you can't afford the time or cost of travel during college, don't worry. Cathy Salgado and Kim Corley waited until they graduated before they went abroad. They traveled for two months with backpacks and Eurail passes, exploring England, Spain, Germany, Switzerland, Italy and Greece. When they returned, Cathy began her job as a sales representative for Procter and Gamble and Kim began her career with IBM.

Howard Sklar graduated from UCLA with a degree in French history, but he didn't think his education was complete. "I'd spent four years cramming my head full of names, dates, literature and facts—but to tell you the truth, I hadn't the slightest idea of what French culture is in real life. I'd never seen it. I'd never lived it."

Howard decided to experience French culture firsthand from the seat of his bicycle. For three weeks he took in the French countryside as he pedaled his way from Paris to Pouilly. Near the end of his trip he finally realized what fascinated him about France. It wasn't the language or the history or the great works of art and literature. Rather, to his surprise, Howard found the heart and soul of France in its wine. Today Howard works as a wine importer in California.

Rich Matteson worked for one year as a restaurant manager after graduating from college before he joined Up With People—the performance organization dedicated to promoting international understanding. After traveling to Belgium, Denmark and Finland, Rich decided to become a full-time staff member with Up With People. He travels all over the world and stays with host families while organizing tours and performing with the cast.

Vince Perez grew up in the Philippines. He had always been interested in international relations, so as a sophomore he applied for a job with the Association for International Students in Business and Economics (AIESEC). Although Vince was from the Philippines, he got a paid job—$1,000 a month—with an American firm in New Jersey. Through an exchange program with Rider College, AIESEC arranged for Vince to live with an American family.

Vince enjoyed the program so much that he became president of the AIESEC for the Philippines. He attended seminars in Australia, Singapore, Belgium and Washington, D.C. Vince's sister joined the same organization and landed a job in Denmark, where she now lives and works.

"AIESEC was my big breakthrough," says Vince, who is director of an international trading firm, Lazard Frères and Company. Vince, who spent the last year working in London, just moved back to New York.

What Do You Learn?

Travel teaches you about other places and other people, but most important it teaches you about yourself.

I spent the fall semester of my junior year in Segovia, Spain, a town of 40,000 sixty-five miles northwest of Madrid. I lived with a Spanish family and attended a local Spanish college, for which I received university credit. I partied with friends from the town (in Spanish) while the other Americans partied (in English) with each other.

On weekends I took the train into Madrid or explored nearby towns. Once my Spanish friend Ma Paz took me outside Segovia to visit her family's village: population, 25. It was out of a storybook. The only building (besides the houses) was a small church where a friar came to say mass each Sunday.

Ma Paz's father, a farmer, lived with her mother in a small house next to a barnyard overflowing with cows. Her grandparents' house was a ten-minute walk away along a patch of gorgeous, rolling hills. They showed me the *bodega* where they made wine from grapes they stomped themselves. Her grandparents were intensely curious about my life back in the United States, asking many questions about my family, my hometown and my university. We talked long into the night.

I felt lucky to meet these generous people. When I reminisce about my semester abroad it's not the Prado, the Alhambra or the eight-hundred-year-old castles that leap to mind first, but my experiences with people such as Ma Paz and her family.

Sue Flynn has similiar feelings about her foreign travels. After graduating from Boston College, she worked for four years before returning to school for a law degree in public service. During that time Sue traveled extensively throughout Europe and South America. "If you can understand and relate to conditions in countries whose people have backgrounds so different from your own, you can come back to the United States and adapt to almost any situation."

What Others Learn About You

A summer or a semester abroad tells a future employer that you have the desire to learn and the courage to explore strange lands. It makes you less of a risk than the untraveled college graduate. International experience also gives you an inside track on overseas assignments.

Where Do You Want to Go?

Maybe you'd like to visit France because you studied French in school or Ireland because your ancestors were Irish. Maybe Canada or Mexico would be the most convenient. Make a list of five countries and the reasons why they interest you.

1.   because

2.   because

3.   because

4.   because

5.   because

If no particular country stands out in your mind as the place you really want to go, take your travel wish list and do some information gathering:

1. Talk to professors
2. Talk to friends who've visited
3. Read whatever you can about the countries

By now you should be passionate about visiting at least a couple of the countries on your wish list. Choose the one that best fits your sense of language, culture and education. Remember, you've got a lifetime to visit every place on your list. Your first extended visit to a foreign country will forever change the way you see yourself and the world. *Vive la expérience!*

How to Get There

Foreign travel is costly. Unless you win a Rotary, Fulbright or Rhodes scholarship, you'll have to come up with the money for the trip yourself.

Here are some low-cost options:

1. You can work in many European countries as an au pair or nanny, taking care of children in the homes of affluent families. In exchange for your services, which may also involve light housework, you receive free room and board and sometimes a small salary.

Advantage: This is a cheap way to get to know another culture. It offers far more than, say, living in a college dorm. Usually you have weekends free to explore the city and surrounding countryside.

Disadvantage: Frequently you do not have the time to venture beyond your immediate surroundings unless you are traveling with the family. The job itself can be quite demanding.

2. You can take a year off from college. I recommend the time between your sophomore and junior years. Work like a dog to save money for the entire first semester and then travel for six months—or as long as your money lasts. You can travel by train with a backpack and visit the main sites in Europe while staying in inexpensive youth hostels. It's best but not essential to travel with a companion.

Advantage: You can plan for and take your trip without any outside interruptions. You can fully immerse yourself in travel: six months is a good chunk of time in which to see several different countries or to concentrate on only one.

Disadvantage: You'll be one year behind your classmates in school. However, this might actually be an advantage, because you'll graduate with more experience than other job applicants. Don't let peer pressure stop you.

3. You can become a Peace Corps volunteer after you graduate from college. This requires a two-year commitment in one of sixty developing nations, working in such areas as nutrition, agriculture, education and hygiene. The salary is a living allowance plus $175 a month for the

time you spend abroad. It is paid in a lump sum after you leave the Corps. Contact your local Peace Corps office for more information or call 1-800-424-8580.

Advantage: If you don't know a foreign language, the Peace Corps will teach you. You'll work with a team of other volunteers in small towns and villages. You'll learn a great deal about developing countries and the people who live there. This is probably one of the most eye-opening experiences abroad.

Disadvantage: The Peace Corps is not for the wary or the uncommitted. Its rewards are not in dollars but in experience.

4. The Peace Corps is only one option for volunteering abroad. The Council on International Educational Exchange—a nonprofit organization of nearly two hundred universities, colleges and youth service agencies—runs service projects in Denmark, Poland, Portugal, Canada, Turkey, Spain and other countries. These two- to four-week programs involve voluntary community service such as renovation of historic sites, forestry and social work in exchange for room and board. For more information, write to: Council on International Educational Exchange, 205 East 42nd Street, New York, N.Y. 10017. There are also long-term service projects, including semester-long programs on Israeli kibbutzim.

Advantage: There's no better way to learn about yourself than through helping others. The personal satisfaction and confidence gained through volunteer work is more than worth your time and effort.

Disadvantage: Unless you choose to volunteer during the summer, you'll lose out on time in school.

5. One of the most common ways to finance international travel is study abroad: for a summer, a semester or a full year. Nearly all colleges sponsor programs abroad for credit, and most of these programs are open to students from other schools. You can also enroll directly in a foreign university in a program designed for foreign students. There are programs in virtually every country. If you really want to study in Finland or Bora Bora, or both, you probably can.

Almost every college features summer and semester abroad programs for credit. Check with your foreign language, art history and humanities departments for details. Perhaps your school has a separate study-abroad office as well. Costs can range from $1,000 for a four-week summer trip to more than $2,500 for a semester of study while living with a host family.

Advantage: This is a great way to learn the language and the culture while earning college credit. If you live with a family abroad, you'll experience the country even more personally.

Disadvantage: Often these programs are very expensive, including airfare and spending money as well as tuition and room and board. Fortunately, most colleges encourage students to apply their financial aid packages to study abroad. There is also the concern that the host family the placement service thought was just right for you might turn out to be less than all you'd hoped for. This is rare: most programs thoroughly screen the families to ensure that they provide a nice home, good food and a pleasant atmosphere for you.

6. Semester at Sea offers students college credit while sailing to several designated countries. Check with your college placement office for details.

Advantage: You are able to see many different countries by way of boat, a thrilling means of travel by anybody's standard. You can also earn up to sixteen units of college credit.

Disadvantage: This is an extremely costly program. Since you are on a boat most of the time, you won't put down roots with people in a particular country. And because most of the students are American, you are essentially transporting America by cruise ship to "wild and exotic places." Some of the adventure is definitely undercut. Finally, instead of traveling by yourself, you are in a group—all the time. "The best way to waste a summer or a semester abroad is to hang out with other Americans," says Susan Finnemore.

7. Of course, there's always the armed services. You're trained in a marketable skill, you get to travel around the world and, when you get out, you'll have the option of continuing your education with a healthy subsidy from Uncle Sam. You might want to consider the ROTC. With this program your undergraduate tuition at a host institution is partially paid for (usually 80 percent). You have the advantage of not worrying about what you're going to be doing once you graduate because you will be fulfilling your obligation to the military (you will serve a minimum of two and a half years). ROTC programs are available for the Army, the Navy and the Air Force. Consult your local recruiter or on-campus ROTC office.

8. Your on-campus travel agency is a great place to shop for bargains. They offer reduced rates on airfares, tours and other travel items. You

can also get an International Student Card, which allows you to visit museums and other attractions worldwide at reduced rates.

9. Try the yellow pages. Inquire about student programs at local travel agencies.

Then again, you just might get a grant or scholarship to study abroad. Marty D'Luzansky taught English in France while on a Fulbright teaching assistantship after he graduated from college with a major in French. He ended up working as a trade consultant with the New Zealand Trade Development Board. "I can't stress enough how important it is to take a year between undergraduate school and whatever it is you think you want to do," he said. "My overseas experience has provided me with the cross-cultural skills essential to help me effectively advise New Zealanders on the best way to succeed with their products or services in the U.S. market. The ability to see the United States from a foreign perspective is critical to my work."

Where to Get the Facts

Many campuses have a foreign travel/exchange office set up to help you. They have information on programs in places as diverse as the Orient, South America and the Soviet Union.

Travel in the United States and Canada

George Washington, who received less formal education than any other President, developed his leadership and people skills early. At twenty-one he went on a mission through the wilderness to carry a warning to the French in the Ohio Valley.

Because Washington took this risk early, he had a tremendous advantage over his colleagues—Jefferson, Adams and Hamilton—who, at this time, had not ventured beyond their own safe territories. They continued to look backward to England and what they knew in the past, while Washington was able, through his travels, to perceive new opportunities in the West.

Maybe your travel in the United States will be in the wilderness of a large metropolitan city, as opposed to the forests that Washington saw, and that's fine. Cities, in many respects, are more wild than the most remote parts of the wilderness. Whichever you decide to investigate, you will develop your sense of adventure and risk taking. Going outside of what you know helps you to become comfortable with the unknown.

What, Specifically, in the United States?

If you cannot afford to travel outside the United States, never fear; there are plenty of activities and programs you can join right on your own campus and in the community which will allow the world to "come to you."

Campus

1. International Students' Organization. Almost every campus has an ISO group where students from around the world join Americans in an exchange of culture, ideas and good times (often centered on delectable cuisine). If there is no such organization on your campus, begin one yourself. Each week someone from a different country gives a speech or slide presentation, followed by refreshments and the opportunity to meet everyone. Also, dinners or banquets are held at which a group of people will prepare their regional cuisine and, perhaps, demonstrate a traditional art or form of dress.

2. International Students' House. You could apply for a job as a clerk at the desk or as a food server at your school's ISH. Or drop by sometime and introduce yourself to several students. Give them your phone number and tell them you would like to get together for lunch or dinner. Remember, they want to learn about America just as much as you want to learn about their culture.

3. Be a volunteer or tutor in English. This is a great way to learn intimately about the culture of a foreign country, through fellow students who become your friends. You can derive a lot of satisfaction from knowing that you are helping to open your culture up to someone else.

Community

1. Work in an ethnic restaurant or in a business run entirely by people from another country. Expose yourself to a different set of customs and values. Ask questions about their home country. How is it different from the United States? How do they perceive Americans? What have they learned from Americans? What has been the biggest cultural barrier?

2. Read the newspapers to find out about international events. Many cities have cultural festivals that feature music, dance and foods from foreign lands. If you have time, get involved in a steering committee to plan such an event. Chances are you'll meet fascinating people from the community who will keep you posted on similar events.

VISTA

VISTA (Volunteers in Service to America) is like the Peace Corps except that the work is done here in the United States. You can work for little or no pay on Indian reservations or in the inner cities of New York, Chicago or San Francisco. Like the Peace Corps, VISTA involves hard work. You must have a strong commitment. Call the VISTA office at (202) 466-4472.

Travel Agencies

Travel agencies also have information on which U.S. cities sponsor international events. And they often offer package tour deals that can make travel a bargain.

Don't Forget . . .

For any type of foreign travel, you'll need a passport. These are available from courts and post offices throughout the country, as well as from designated passport agencies in most major cities. You'll also need a visa for travel to most Eastern European countries, as well as to France. For visa information, you can contact the country's embassy or write to the Office of Passport Services, Room 386, 1425 K Street, N.W., Washington, D.C. 20524, for "visa requirements."

Other Horizons

There are many ways to enrich your travel experience before, during and after your trip. Brushing up on the language, reading about the history of the country and learning about the people before you go can make you feel more at home right from the start.

Let's say you've chosen to visit France. Before your trip, you may want to listen to some French-language tapes and practice the most commonly used phrases. (It helps if you've studied the language in school, but it's not essential.) What are other considerations?

Art

> Every region of the world has its own unique art forms. You may want to research the region you intend to visit.

Literature

> Read works by native authors as an entertaining way to learn about the country you are visiting.

History

> Invest in a paperback on the country's history so that the sights you see will have greater significance for you.

Music

> Listen to local radio stations during your trip. This will help you understand the language and expose you to the country's music.

Philosophy

> Who were the philosophers that influenced cultural development? How has their thinking affected everyday life?

Politics and Economics

> Think about the way the country is governed. How does it differ from the United States? What are the pluses and minuses? What is the economic system?

Business

> What is the local commerce? What are the major industries? Is the country rich in natural resources, human resources, agriculture or technological advances? What American companies thrive in the country?

No matter where you plan to go, from Peru to Japan, getting a sense of the country beforehand will help you feel better upon arrival. You can learn and adapt on the road by carrying a guidebook as a useful reference and road map.

Below, you'll find an "information sheet" which you might want to fill in before your trip. Don't worry if you are unable to fill in most of the blanks; that's why you're taking the trip.

TRAVEL INFORMATION SHEET for _____

History (thumbnail sketch of major events)

Art and architectural contributions (four or five major works, artists)

Scientific and technological contributions

Cultural, religious and philosophical movements

Intellectual and literary contributions

Political climate (past and present)

Social and economic conditions

This is only a partial list. Don't stop here! Make foreign or domestic travel a goal. It may be the most valuable thing you do during your college years.

The use of travelling is to regulate the imagination by reality and, instead of thinking how things may be, to see them as they are.

SAMUEL JOHNSON

▪ 9 ▪

NETWORKING
Mapping Out Your
Career Strategy

The need to be opportunistic, to think on your feet, again underscores the importance of tuning in to people—of hearing not only what they say but the larger and underlying meaning as well.

MARK McCORMACK,
What They Don't Teach You at Harvard Business School

"**D**on't wait for the business connections to come to you," says Chris Salgado, an operations manager at Morgan Guaranty. "You have to talk to as many people as possible and don't be afraid of asking questions. The more aggressive you are at asking questions, the more information you'll have on which to make a decision." By visiting his school's career placement office when he was a sophomore, Chris had the competitive advantage over his classmates who waited until the eleventh hour to investigate career contacts.

In business, meeting people, gathering information, following up and building relationships are among the most important things you can do. Skills with people can make the difference between landing a job and getting a form letter thanking you for your time. The common terms for these skills are "courtesy" and "concern"; yuppies call it "networking." Don't be put off. Networking has some important points to recommend it to anyone preparing to take the plunge into the professional world.

Think of networking as savvy with a social conscience. "Be gutsy," advises Nancy Forsyth. "You can't expect people to help you out if you don't do something for yourself." Nancy, a business graduate from the University of New Hampshire, built strong relationships with her professors and the counselors at the placement office. "Your mentors

123

in college have the best connections and they care about helping you assess what you should do," says Nancy, now in marketing for the Boston publisher Allyn & Bacon. "But students must make the initial effort to seek these people out."

Keep in mind that contacts are everywhere, in the classroom and out, in the office and out. "You've got to be around to get around," says David Herndon, *New York Newsday* features editor. After graduating from Columbia's Graduate School of Journalism, David had to spend three years doing odd jobs (including compiling sections for an encyclopedia, which was "like writing high school book reports") before he finally got his break. Ironically, it came from a former fellow student who had landed a job with *Sport* magazine and asked David to write a few articles. David did, and was then recommended for a job as sports editor at *The Village Voice*. He got the job, and over the next five years he made up for lost time, moving from sports editor to managing editor (at age twenty-nine) to features editor for *New York Newsday*. Although he had been a highly qualified student, editor of his college magazine and voted "Most Likely to Succeed in Journalism," David found that getting that first good job is not just a matter of talent and hard work; it also involves "circumstance and opportunity."

In *The Achievement Factors*, B. Eugene Griessman writes: "Opportunities are usually for the moment, and as they pass by, there is often only a brief moment to grab them."

The Search

Why not use your career search as a launching pad for networking skills? For career search purposes, networking basically means contacting people who can:

1. Tell you about a specific job
2. Get you in touch with someone "important" at a company that interests you
3. Keep you in mind for potential future jobs
4. Hire you
5. Provide you with inside information
6. Introduce you to someone who can give you valuable information
7. Coach you in your career pursuit

Why is networking—or making career and business contacts—so important? For one thing, you need people contacts, whether you're looking for a job or not. (Your grade-point average will not always be your best friend.) Second, you need people to tell you firsthand how to make the transition from college student to job applicant. Talking to people about this transition will be more helpful than reading ten books on "how to get the job of your dreams."

In fields like finance, connections can be everything. John Carrigan, thirty, has his own seat on the Chicago Board of Trade. He says his first contact in the field was made through a friend from high school. John was a runner in the grain room working for Conti Commodities during college. His three summer internships and the contacts he made were a foot in the door for his first post-college job trading futures for Paine Webber.

First Things First

You've balanced your academic, extracurricular and real-world experience. Now you must develop a game plan to achieve your career goals.

Where to Begin

First, take inventory of your summer internships and part-time jobs. Did the work interest you? What do you most value from your college classes and activities?

Use those answers to help you decide which jobs interest you most. Then talk to people who have those jobs now. This should sound familiar to you since you've been "networking" with your professors, friends and business contacts since your freshman year.

If possible, ask your networking contacts if you can observe them on the job. Tell them that you want to get an accurate picture of a typical workday. Would you work alone or with others? Would you be closely supervised or independent? What environment would you work in? Would you travel?

Cultivating Contacts Now and in the Future

Much of your success in business will depend on the relationships you have with other people. If you learn early to pick people's brains and to incorporate their successful qualities, you will be far ahead of your contemporaries. You have much to learn from your role models in business, but you have as much to learn from all of your other business associates.

Networking doesn't mean merely making yourself visible to those in a position to give you a promotion, though that is important. It also means cultivating relationships with all the people behind the scenes, the people who actually get things done—the receptionist, mail clerk, messenger, office manager, janitor—people whose jobs go mostly unrecognized by the corporate hierarchy. Good relationships with the people under you, as well as those above you, can ensure your own success. Networking involves a willingness to learn anything from anyone who works with you, in *any* capacity.

Business Week columnist Paul Nadler says he always sends postcards to the office's photocopying personnel. He depends heavily on quick and efficient photocopies, especially at deadline time.

Building relationships with all kinds of people will help you if you ever want to be in management. As a manager, you are a leader, organizing, inspiring and working with others to achieve professional and personal goals. How do you learn the principles of good management?

"Not by reading about great leaders whose experience is so foreign it makes it impossible to identify with them," says Andrew S. Grove, CEO of Intel Corporation, in a *Fortune* article. Grove won't endorse wilderness excursions or white-water rafting as the secret to management success. Good leadership and good management are learned "the same way each of us has learned the important, unteachable roles in our lives, be they that of husband or wife, father or mother: by studying the behavior of people who have made a success of it and modeling ourselves after them."

Networking means learning from others. It also means being a teacher to others when you have the knowledge, experience and expertise to give someone else guidance.

John Goode and Elizabeth Bastion were hired right out of graduate school by a major financial newsweekly. Each held an entry-level editorial position. John was eager to learn, inquisitive and helpful to co-workers in his training seminar. When Ann was having a hard time figuring out the ATEX computer system, John took the time to sit down and help her. He wasn't much more experienced than she, but he figured he'd learn by helping. When they couldn't resolve a glitch, John was the one who went to the seminar instructor and asked for help. Not only was he happy to help them figure out the problem, but he became interested in the sample article they were working on. And he was impressed with John's editorial eye. This gave John the opportunity to get to know a senior editor in an informal situation, sincerely and without any grandstanding.

Elizabeth had a different approach. During this seminar she was constantly interrupting the other trainees, interjecting her "considered opinion" based on her "vast experience" working at her father's newspaper in a midsize Midwestern city. She name-dropped. When Ann asked to talk with her about her experiences, Elizabeth raised her head and, with a bored expression, said she'd love to if she had the time, but right now she was "consumed" with a special feature proposal for the magazine.

At promotion time, Elizabeth was laboring on her still uncommissioned special feature while John was promoted to assistant managing editor with responsibility for developing a financial news column for college graduates. The senior editors believed John would be a better long-term choice because he was a superior teacher, listener, communicator and motivator. He was a role model. Elizabeth was . . . well . . . She returned to her midsize Midwestern city to work on her father's newspaper.

The moral is staring you in the face.

How Have You Networked?

Have you "networked" on your summer internship or part-time job? Even if you have only waited on tables through college, think of how your success depended on your co-workers. Seriously.

An excellent waiter who is liked and respected by his co-workers is far more effective—and therefore more profitable—than the average waiter. Why? Because if the host or hostess likes him, he'll get his tables turned (cleared off and set) faster than the others. If the cook likes him, he'll get occasional special orders for his "preferred" customers. If the manager realizes how valuable his work and his good disposition are, he or she will make special arrangements—like letting him work as much or as little as he wants to accommodate his school schedule—just to keep him. Finally, the customer—the ultimate recipient of this entire team process—stands a greater chance of being pleased with the service. Therefore this waiter will probably get a better tip—one of his goals in the first place.

Good human relations will help you in any job. Some people have a natural knack for dealing with people; others have a hard time. If you are in the latter category, take heart. There are ways of gaining confidence that will help you to understand people better—how you relate to them and how they relate to you.

The classic on this subject is *How to Win Friends and Influence People* by Dale Carnegie. He outlines six basic principles for successful interaction. (There's so much common sense here that it's easy to take this formula for granted. Don't.)

1. Become genuinely interested in other people
2. Smile
3. Remember that a person's name is to that person the sweetest and most important sound in any language
4. Be a good listener. Encourage others to talk about themselves
5. Talk in terms of other people's interests
6. Make the other person feel important and do it sincerely

Networking is a new word for, among other things, effective human relations. Good manners, sincerity, a positive attitude and a winning spirit mean good business. They always have, and they always will.

Mentors

Get yourself a mentor. As I said earlier, a mentor is a teacher, a coach, a guide—somebody you have a rapport with and a respect for, preferably in your chosen career field. A mentor is sometimes a model and other times a teacher. (Whitey Herzog was a mediocre baseball player but has become one of the game's most successful managers.)

Cynthia Harris was lucky. She found her mentor without even trying. Cynthia was a secretary at a Merrill Lynch branch office. She had never gone to college; nor had anyone in her family. One day her boss, Joe Pachinsky, took Cynthia to lunch for a heart-to-heart talk.

"You have too much potential to stay in this job," he told her. "There's no limit to what you can do."

Cynthia asked Joe if he thought she could make it in college.

"Absolutely," he replied. "As much as I would hate to see you leave, it's necessary for your own growth and development."

Four months later, Cynthia quit her job and enrolled in college as a nursing major. A year later, she switched her major to rehabilitation. She did a summer internship in Chicago's inner city, joined a sorority and did volunteer work with cancer patients and abused children. Four years after giving her resignation to Joe, Cynthia graduated—with honors.

Today, Cynthia is a top-notch social worker in Chicago. She insists that without the help of Joe, her mentor, she would still be pushing papers from nine to five in her hometown, daydreaming about college.

A Mentor Made in Heaven?

So how will you meet your mentor? Will he or she appear to you magically? Probably not. You must seek mentors out, and in doing so, you'll be helping to define yourself. Which professors most inspire you? Talk to them after class. Ask them for special assignments. Perhaps your mentor will be among the management at the office where you have a part-time job or a summer internship.

To be effective at networking, you must first examine your own personality. Think about those people you most admire (professors, movie stars, politicians, characters from literature, etc.). Think about the people who've had the greatest (positive) influence on you. What distinguishes them from the rest of the herd? Why do they appeal to you? Learn how to ask questions of the people you work with who have more experience and more knowledge than you do. Why do they stand out? Watch them in action. Analyze what they do.

Baltimore *Sun* New York bureau chief Thomas Easton found his career shaped dramatically by a mentor. In college he was reluctant to specialize in any one area. He was interested in everything, from film to history to political science. When he graduated, he had a vague idea that his broad range of interests might make him suitable for journalism, but he wasn't sure. Then on a job interview for a chain of Connecticut weekly newspapers he met editor John Peterson, who had won awards as an investigative reporter. The two hit it off right way. Peterson's great curiosity and energy matched Easton's. "I asked him once if he wanted to go out for coffee," Easton says, laughing. "And he said, 'No, I didn't hire you to get coffee. I hired you to get stories. Get out there.' " Because of his mentor, Easton made an extraordinary career jump. After two years on the weekly, he worked for a daily for six months, went to business school and ended up on one of the best papers in the country. Easton says the *Sun* weighed two things heavily: his business degree, and a stellar recommendation from Peterson.

One other thing: it's important that your mentor be someone you can get to know. If you want to be a playwright, Shakespeare might be ideal, but he's dead. Why not cultivate a relationship with the playwriting professor at your local college?

The Mentor Dynamic

How does the mentor-protégé relationship come about in the working world? In business you will have certain people whom you look up to and admire more than others. It may be your boss, but it could just as easily be someone in a different department with whom you've worked on a specific project.

If someone takes a special interest in you because you have been an apprentice to them—taking on extra assignments, staying late to help on a special project, etc.—they are more likely to give you advice. They may tell you how to best prepare yourself for a promotion. Or they may have detailed suggestions on how to do your present job more efficiently.

In addition to learning more about the job you are doing, your mentor or mentors learn more about *you*. They are able to see you functioning in a number of different capacities in and out of your job description, and they are more likely to go to bat for you at salary and/or promotion time.

To have a mentor-protégé relationship and to actually learn from those people who can teach you, you must be eager to learn. Ditch any attitude of arrogance. It won't get you anywhere. I'm not saying don't be confident—you have to believe in yourself—but have the wisdom to know what you can learn from others.

The Essentials

Below are some essential characteristics which you should have regardless of what you do. Take stock. Which best describe you? Which don't describe you? How might you improve your weak areas before you graduate?

supportive	sets goals
decisive	keeps his or her word
follows up	has long-term vision
organized	sense of humor
ethical	positive attitude
sets and keeps high standards	
confident, but not cocky	
fair, winning attitude	ability to separate the trivial from the important
honest	
able to manage stress	
even-tempered	
generous	
works well with all kinds of people	
pays attention to detail	

If you evaluate yourself, you'll be well prepared for your first salary review when your manager discusses your performance. And you'll accept constructive criticism more easily. You can't become better at something if you don't know what you need to improve.

Other Contacts

Throughout college, you've pushed yourself to branch out, experience new things, meet people and ask questions. Beginning in your junior year, narrow your focus to the career you think you want to pursue.

Here are some good people to contact:

1. Company representatives who've registered with your career placement office
2. Company recruiters listed in the College Placement Annual (this is revised yearly and is available at the placement office)
3. Members of your school's alumni office who are in fields you want to pursue
4. Professionals in your hometown
5. Professors at your university
6. Your parents' friends, your siblings or their friends
7. Authors of books you've read in your field of interest
8. People who have given speeches in your career area

Of course, this is only a partial listing, but it should at least get you started. Keep a checklist of important people you want to meet to gather information. Try to meet and speak with one key person a month during your junior and senior years. Keep notes on your conversations so that you can make comparisons and analyze the advice you're given.

How Do You Contact Key People?

To get to the "key" person, you must first make a good impression on the person in the real power seat: the secretary or assistant.

Treat the secretary with as much respect—or more—than the other people you intend to interview. Tell him why you would like to see the director of X and show him your résumé. Explain why you are interested in the company and talk about your experiences and abilities. Ask for information on the company so that you can study it before your interview.

The secretary is the eyes and ears for the person you need to speak with. He is skilled at knowing exactly what his boss values and looks for, so he is the first in the chain of people to win over.

If the secretary does not grant you the interview, be gracious. Thank him for his time and send follow-up letters to the key person and to the secretary with whom you spoke, restating your interest. Often the initial "no" is a smokescreen. Your diplomatic, consistent follow-up may secure the interview.

Meeting someone in person always leaves the best impression. How easily you can set up a meeting will depend on where you live and the level of competition in the industry. If you are in a large metropolitan city where business people's schedules are packed every day, you will have a more difficult time. If you are in a city with a moderate business pace, people will probably be more accessible. Be professional, courteous and direct. State your interest and your reasons for wanting to interview them. (This is crucial with a professional whom you have not met previously.) Be poised and well dressed. You'll probably have only two to three minutes to set up the lunch appointment or half-hour meeting (see the following sample interview to set up the appointment).

First Interview:

YOU: Hello, Ms. Marshall. Thank you for taking time to see me today.

KEY PERSON: My pleasure. What can I do for you?

YOU: As your assistant probably told you, I am one year away from graduating with a degree in architectural design. Since your firm has designed some of the most outstanding buildings in this state, I wanted to express an interest early in working with you someday.

I wondered, specifically, if I might be able to set up a luncheon appointment with you or one of your junior associates so that I could learn firsthand about the qualities you seek in graduates you hire as first-year associates.

KP: I admire your foresight. Unfortunately, I am swamped right now and would not be able to take out two hours to meet with you. However, there is one exemplary employee who has worked for us for two years and who graduated from your program. His name is Jordan Simon and he may be available to give you some advice.

YOU: I would appreciate speaking with him. Thank you very much for your time. I hope we are able to see each other in the next year.

KP: You're welcome. My assistant will be happy to give you Jordan's phone number. He manages our other office. Tell him I sent you.
            Good luck.

Phone Interview with Jordan:

YOU: Jordan, I am a junior at State A&M and will graduate next year with a degree in Architectural Design. Cynthia Marshall recommended that I speak with you to get some advice on how I might best prepare to work for your firm someday. May I take you to lunch sometime next week so we can talk further?

JORDAN: I exercise at lunch every day, but I'd be happy to meet you for breakfast if you tell me why it would be worth my time.

YOU: Gladly. I have a 3.6 GPA and two summers of experience working for your competitors and have put myself through school. I am a hard worker and a team player, and I have a very creative mind. I'd like to speak with you in person to pick your brains and find out how you think, plan and organize your time.

JORDAN: (Interrupting) That's a good start. Where and when would you like to get together?

Before the actual interview, make a list of good questions to ask. You shouldn't be doing all the talking. You should be listening and asking what else you can do to prepare for success. Be confident but don't be cocky. You may end up with an apprenticeship which can get you in the door at graduation time.

You are now narrowing the options of your career pursuit. On the basis of all the information you've gathered over the last three years, limit your choices to two or three areas.

If you have strong people skills and you want to be in management someday, sales may be the place to start. If you're strong in information, you may want to begin in an entry-level market research position. If you're strong in the area of objects, you may want to begin as an apprentice with a craftsperson or professional in your technical area of interest.

Getting the Word Out

Whom do you contact? Anyone and everyone who is even remotely related to your selected career and job. If you can't think of at least five people to contact, you're not thinking hard enough.

If a contact gives you a specific name, ask permission to use his or her name as a reference. Some people may decide to call on your behalf. Enlist their support.

Gathering Information

With each contact you make, take notes on their responses. Ask whom else you could contact to advise you. If at all possible, thank people with a short note.

If an interview follows from a contact you've made, remember that you still have to be the best candidate among those competing for the job. You must be just as prepared, well rehearsed and qualified for the job as the next applicant.

For those companies which interest you most, you may want to write down the names of people who could give you valuable information about that company or the field. Then interview these people and ask them questions that you consider important. What are the pros and cons of the industry? Of that company? Of the company's philosophy? What does and doesn't appeal to them? What have they liked/disliked the most? This will be your "Career Strategy" sheet and it will help you assess whether the field and the job are right for you. Below is an example.

Career Strategy

Field: Banking
Job: Management trainee
Contact people in banking:
1. Entry level
2. Upper management
3. Former employees
4. Alumni in banking
Learn more about the job:
1. Day-to-day work
2. Career opportunities
3. Work environment
List of questions I want to ask:

Before you interview the individuals who will give you the real story on the company, brainstorm a list of potential candidates you'd like to speak with. You may not get to talk to all of them, but writing down their names will let you figure out whose advice may have the greatest impact. For instance, who has the most important job in the company? Who, despite their level, is most happy in his or her job? Why? Is it the company, or is it that person's approach to the job, or a combination of both? Questioning as many people as possible in a very diplomatic way will give you volumes of information with which to make a good decision.

Network Map: Chart It Out!

SYLVIA ROBINSON
Alumni
V.P., Interstate Bank

CHARLES DEAN
President
Hometown Bank

AL RUBEN
V.P., Finance

JOHN SLOAN
Credit Card
Manager

MARK GIBB
Financial Planner
Merrill Lynch

MARY ROLATTA
Ex-employee;
now has own
business

ANNE GIBB
Teller

Career Network Map

Field:

Job:

Contact people:

   1. Entry level   a.

                             b.

                             c.

   2. Upper management   a.

                             b.

                             c.

   3. Former employees   a.

                             b.

                             c.

   4. Alumni who are   a.
      now in the field

                             b.

                             c.

Impressions of the industry:

PROS   CONS

    There you have it. Networking involves far more than just meeting people and gathering information. It's a two-way street. Sure, you will gain a lot from others, but not unless you're prepared to contribute as well. If you can't help someone directly, at least be prepared to thank them in earnest for their support. And when you can, help others who are less experienced than you. Take pleasure in knowing that you're being a mentor or role model just as others have been for you.

·10·

PAPERWORK
Résumés, Cover Letters and the Job Application

Thought is the soul of act.
ROBERT BROWNING

Brevity is the soul of wit.
WILLIAM SHAKESPEARE

I know, I know. Résumés are boring, there's no getting around it. The consolation prize is that, by continual self-assessment, you've been developing your résumé since your freshman year. You won't have to worry so much about becoming comatose when confronted with the need for "action" verbs like "generated," "coordinated," etc., etc.

Now for the straight scoop on résumés: a bad résumé may lose you a job and a good résumé won't get you one. It's not supposed to. The goal of a good résumé is to get the interview. It's a springboard for a prospective employer's questions. And, later, it's a reminder on file of who you are.

Worst-Case Scenario

"Oh yeah, I remember Alisha Bitterroot . . . the one with the musk-scented, floral-bordered fuchsia-colored résumé spelled 're-ZOO-may.' "

This chapter is designed to help you avoid these costly, albeit amusing, mistakes.

First Impressions

A résumé should be written with the craftiness required when trying to get out of a parking ticket for running a red light. Or when getting dressed for a date. You choose clothes that accentuate some features and downplay others to express a mood appropriate to the occasion. (You don't alter your features—you just make the good ones look better.)

Résumés are hard to write because they must be simple. We're talking bare bones here. Your résumé should favorably convey in one page your education, job history, activities and achievements while being clear, concise and honest. List items in chronological order, beginning with the most recent. Give your name, address, phone number and job objective. List any skills relevant to your employment—foreign languages, secretarial skills, whatever. Your résumé should offer—but not include—personal references on request.

Your résumé should be targeted for a specific position. If you're applying for several different jobs, you need résumés for each one. One size does *not* fit all.

To get your résumé noticed, you'll need an ace cover letter. A what? A form letter covering the résumé with a curling arrow and a boldface message reading RÉSUMÉ BELOW followed by a full line of exclamation points?

!!

That might not be such a bad idea but, unfortunately, this is not the kind of cover letter most employers have come to expect. The cover letter is not the domain of the pioneer abstract expressionist avant-garde existentialist career hunter. Not as of this writing anyway.

The cover letter lets you do two things: herald your résumé and obtain the interview. Your cover letter will convince the reader to turn the page and pay attention to the résumé. It needs to be good, so take just as much care in preparing it as you do your résumé.

Your cover letter should:

1. Express interest in the company and a specific position
2. Engage the reader's attention so he or she is compelled to turn the page and read your résumé
3. Mention a specific date when, if they have not contacted you, you will contact them

The cover letter "covers" the shortcomings of the résumé form. At its best, it becomes a narrative version of most of the information contained in that, well, boring résumé. You can take the highlights of your achievements and personalize them. This adds some humanity to the cold facts on your résumé. Of equal importance, the cover letter provides you with the opportunity to discuss the particular company to which you're applying. You can and often should mention something specifically appealing about the prospective employer. This lets the "personal approach" work in two directions—yours and theirs. And it makes things much more interesting.

The COVER LETTER should appeal visually. Type it up on personalized stationery, if possible. Get a correcting ribbon—no correction fluid! Briefly state your most compelling qualifications, then mention the appeal the company has for you. Request an interview.

Says *New York Newsday* features editor David Herndon: Give the letter some zing. Don't dwell on the reasons why it would be a good experience for you to work for the prospective employer. "Tell him why it would be a good experience for *him* to work with you." Follow up with a phone call in two weeks.

THANK-YOU NOTES following interviews are neither necessary nor expected—all the more reason why it's so important to send them. They need not be elaborate. Just say thanks.

And then there's the JOB APPLICATION. Like your other work papers, it should be neat and well thought out. If you can, fill the application out at home. Before writing on the actual application, write your responses on scratch paper. That way, you can refine your thoughts before committing them to paper where you won't be able to make changes.

On pages 147–150 there is an extremely comprehensive job application. Fill it out for practice. Look at your responses later and see what you think. Are you crisp and to the point? Are your examples convincing? Would you be interested in interviewing someone like you based on your application? ("Absolutely NOT . . ." Just kidding, you say.)

Sample Cover Letter

Melanie McFadden
9 Circle Street
Columbus, Ohio 08032

April 10, 1990

Mr. James Ward
Director of Operations
Database International
5510 Mainway Drive
Los Angeles, CA 92380

Dear Mr. Ward:

I am a senior majoring in computer science and information processing at the University of Florida.

I am keenly interested in your company because of your first-rate products, especially the DB SX1000 system, which I have used for the past two years. More than any other company I've researched, Database has set the standard for quality and innovation in sales and technology.

Enclosed is my résumé outlining my academic, extracurricular and work experience for the past four years. As you can see, I've worked hard to learn firsthand about the computer industry.

If you would like to call me to set up a personal interview, I can be reached at (216) 898-3452. If I don't hear from you by Monday, April 30, I'll call you.

Thank you for your consideration. I look forward to hearing from you soon.

Sincerely,

Melanie McFadden

Sample Résumé

MELANIE McFADDEN

9 Circle Street

Columbus, Ohio 08032

(216) 898-3452

JOB OBJECTIVE: Position as programmer with supervisory responsibilities

WORK EXPERIENCE:

* Anderson, Inc., 1989 to present—worked 20 hours per week as a programmer for privately owned company.

* Tutor, University of Florida, Computer Science Center—worked by the hour with students who needed further help at the freshman and sophomore levels.

* Borrans Corporation: summer intern—programmer, operations trainee responsible for training new employees and experienced employees in need of additional instruction.

EDUCATION:

* Computer science/information processing major; liberal arts minor. University of Florida.
  GPA: 3.4.

* Junior semester abroad: Florence, Italy. Studied history, art, music, Renaissance literature and Italian.

* Rotary scholarship finalist: May 1989. Alternate for one year of travel in Fife, Scotland.

ACTIVITIES/HONORS:

* Vice President, College Democrats: 1988–89. Recruited students to participate in 1989 city, state and local campaigns.

* Treasurer, Campus Achievers: 1987–88. Student service honorary.

* President, 1987–88, Student Union Activities Board—coordinated various activities, including Parents' Day and spring vacations.

References available on request.

Sample Thank-You Note

Melanie McFadden
9 Circle Street
Columbus, Ohio 08032
(216) 898-3452
May 7, 1990

Mr. James Ward
Director of Operations
Database International
5510 Mainway Drive
Los Angeles, CA 92380

Dear Mr. Ward:

Thank you for taking the time to talk with me about entry-level programming positions at Database International.

After our discussion, I am still most interested in working with the DB SX1000 system, though the others you mentioned sounded challenging as well. If it is convenient for you, I would like to set up an appointment to visit the plant so that I can speak with people in the different divisions we discussed. I am eager to see the specifics of the jobs you outlined and find out about career paths within Database International.

If I don't hear from you by the end of the week, I will call you on May 14. I have several job possibilities with other companies, but I am most interested in your company and your unique, trendsetting products.

Again, thank you for your time and consideration. It was a pleasure to meet you.

Sincerely,

Melanie McFadden

Sample Résumé

GEORGE RAPPAPORT

154 West 78th Street

New York, NY 10024

JOB OBJECTIVE: Entry-level public accounting position with medium-to large-size firm.

WORK EXPERIENCE:

* Internal Auditor, 1986 to present, HealthCare Insurance Agency, Baltimore, MD. Managed nine corporate accounts. Responsible for training and supervising staff of twelve.

* Summer Intern, 1987, Kenase Accountants—twenty-person office—experienced a small firm firsthand. Managed four of the company's ten largest accounts as well as eighteen long-term clients.

* Summer Intern, 1986—Business Management Legal Associates—worked in the legal accounting and tax department for partners and associates.

EDUCATION:

*   Accounting major, English minor, University of Maryland, 1988. GPA: 3.6.

*   Dean's List—six semesters

*   Junior semester in Mexico City, Mexico. Studied Spanish and Mexican heritage while living with a Mexican family.

ACTIVITIES:

*   Volunteer—Big Brother Program—1986–88. Worked as a coach and a one-on-one "big brother" with two underprivileged teenagers.

*   President, Blue Key, 1988—National Senior Honorary

*   Scholarship Chairman, Phi Kappa Psi Fraternity

References available on request.

Think of résumé writing and the job search preparation as "marketing" yourself. You want to give the best impression possible in what may be a two-second period of time. The way you dress, speak and follow up is all part of your self-promotion. Again, you may see a key person only briefly, but you want to make a lasting, winning impression. And you will.

Please print in ink. Attach separate sheets if necessary.

Name First, Middle, Last	Social Security No.

Home Address Street City State Zip	Home Phone

How long at present address?	Are you in the U.S. on a temporary visa?

In emergency, notify (name/address/phone)

List any friends or relatives working with the company, by name and relationship.

Have you ever applied for work here before? If so, when?

Do you own or have access to a car?	Has your license ever been suspended or revoked? If so, why?

EDUCATION

High School		College
Name of school, date entered, location		
Graduation date and grade point average		
List major and minor fields		
Scholastic honors		
Any academic or disciplinary problems? If yes, explain.		
List extracurricular or athletic activities.		
Part-time jobs.		
How did you spend your summer vacations?		
Are you proud of your college record?		

WORK EXPERIENCE
From / Through / Most recent employer / May we contact?
Address   Phone
Current or final supervisor
Starting position and salary
How did you get the job?   Why did you leave?
What did you like the best about the job?
What did you like least about the job?
From / Through / employer before No. 1 / May we contact?
Address   Phone
Current or final supervisor
Starting position and salary
How did you get the job?   Why did you leave?
What did you like the best about the job?
Wht did you like least about the job?
Please summarize any relevant experience which uniquely qualifies you for this job.

REFERENCES

List three persons, not relatives or former employers, who have known you for the last five years whom we may contact.

	NAME	ADDRESS	YEARS KNOWN
1.			
2.			
3.			

State your own personal definition of this position:

Please tell us why you want this job and why you think you would be successful.

ACTIVITIES

Excluding religious or political groups, with what organizations do you now work?

What are your hobbies?

What magazines or newspapers do you read? Why do they interest you?

How many hours do you watch TV per week?

What types of books do you read most often?

What do you consider your most important accomplishment?

What has been your most serious disappointment?

Describe the most competitive situation you've been in and the steps you took to achieve success.

What do you consider to be your three most important assets?

What are your greatest weaknesses?
Are you willing to travel? To relocate?
When can you start to work?
At this time, how many interviews have you arranged and in what fields?
Is there any additional information which you consider important?

·11·

YOUR THIRD DEGREE
Interviews

The worst thing you can possibly do in a deal [or interview] is seem desperate to make it. That makes the other guy smell blood and then you're dead. The best thing you can do is deal from strength, and leverage is the biggest strength you have. Leverage is having what the other guy wants. Or better yet, needs. Or best of all, simply can't do without.
DONALD TRUMP, *The Art of the Deal*

"Like making a deal, there is a special art to interviewing," says Anne Marie Myers, who coaches people on how to prepare for interviews. "You have to convince the prospective employer that they need you to work for their company. But to do that, you have to first convince yourself." Ninety percent of the interview, Myers says, is based on the confidence and image you project.

So what's the worst that can happen during an interview?

When asked to describe how you function under pressure, you let out a high-pitched shriek, double over in your chair and laugh uncontrollably—so hard, in fact, that tears roll down your face and soil your new blouse. Unable to breathe, you gasp periodically. The recruiter, visibly frightened, buzzes the secretary at her outer alcove and asks for a box of Kleenex, which the secretary does not have and so is asked, in an imperative panic, *to find* . . .

In place of hysteria you are stricken with amnesia:

RECRUITER: Tell me about yourself.
YOU: Who?
RECRUITER: You . . . yourself. Tell me about yourself.
YOU: I don't remember.
RECRUITER: Well, Barbara, thank you for your time. We'll be in touch.
YOU: Barbara?

If the above scenarios seem unlikely, you can relax about interviewing for your first big job. The more typical ways of fouling up during interviews—which *everybody* has, at some point, done—are far less embarrassing and much easier to correct.

Sarah Greenspan's first interview demonstrates what can happen to a good candidate who starts off unprepared. Sarah is hardworking, outgoing, smart, athletic—generally and specifically on the ball. The kind of person you dream of being.

Sarah's first-choice company was Xerox. Their corporate headquarters is located on the East Coast, near her hometown. The company philosophy was one she admired, and the starting salary for sales reps was very attractive indeed. Sarah was, in a word, psyched.

But, as you may have guessed, psyched was not enough. The problem was that Sarah was too *much* psyched and too *little* prepared. Because she was uninformed, unrehearsed and unprepared, the recruiter spent only fifteen minutes with her despite impressive credentials—top of her class, student body vice president and an employee of the campus copy center. What do I mean by "unprepared"? Back to Sarah.

XEROX: Sarah, I'd be interested to know a little about how you've overcome defeat.

SARAH: Well, um, let me think. I tend to be pretty successful when I put my mind to something. I guess there was the time when I was running for homecoming queen. I lost. And I mean, I was really busy, it was my junior year. I was student body vice president, I was working part-time at the campus copy center (we had Xerox machines, by the way), and I guess I didn't really have the time to devote to promoting myself the way I would have liked. I mean, I still think I could have won. But I got over it.

This was minute seven of the interview process. By minute fourteen, Sarah was thanked for her time and ushered to the door. What was wrong with Sarah's response?

First, Sarah was out of sync. She was still trying to sell her invincible being when the recruiter was specifically asking for a candid discussion of failure. She wasn't listening.

And perhaps because she wasn't listening, the rest of her response sounded scattered and insincere. That wasn't the moment to plug Xerox; the recruiter had her résumé, so he knew she'd worked with their photocopiers and was familiar with the product. What he was looking for was Sarah's response to defeat—*real* defeat. He wanted to see her capacity to evaluate herself under adverse circumstances and her ability to do something constructive.

How so? Back to Sarah, this time under better circumstances, in her interview with Gallo, where she was subsequently offered a job.

GALLO: How have you overcome defeat?

SARAH: Well, I very much wanted a university fellowship for a year's study abroad. I had been thinking about a career in international relations; I wanted to see Europe and I knew I probably wouldn't have another chance to immerse myself in a foreign culture. I put all my eggs in one basket. I didn't apply for any other study-abroad programs, and in April, after the second interview, I was nixed. Despite being seriously disappointed, I regrouped. I contacted the International Council on Economic Development and found out about volunteer programs in Latin America. I worked at the campus copy center that summer, saving money, getting work experience and taking my mind off "what I didn't get." That fall I immersed myself in Latin American studies and applied for the Council's volunteer program in Bolivia. I was accepted, and the following May I was off. I think now that this was the best I could have hoped for. I was able to help other people and at the same time learned self-reliance. I found out about the world and myself.

Notice the difference in Sarah's response. She didn't try to dodge the question or "reframe" it to suit her agenda. She was clear, while showing the capacity for reflection and honest self-appraisal. She was also able to tell a lot about herself without blowing her own horn. The recruiter could deduce motivation, tenacity, concern for others and self-reliance. He could see complexity and capability from a response that lasted only ninety seconds. He liked what he saw and made her an offer. (Sarah also received offers from Lever Brothers and Carnation.)

Let's look at another example. Alan King was extremely well qualified and well prepared for his interview with Shearson Lehman Hutton. He had researched the company and the position, he had spoken with several employees and he did an excellent job of communicating his background and his career aspirations. But when the interviewer wrapped up the conversation, he said, "Alan, you have excellent credentials and I'm sure you'll be very successful when you begin your career. However, I don't think you're what we're looking for here."

Alan, thinking on his feet, said, "If Shearson is seeking employees who are quick starters, inquisitive, hardworking, dedicated and committed to making things happen, then you should hire me. If you want an employee who won't be dissuaded by obstacles or excuses and if you want someone who will continually lead others in finding new and creative ways to solve problems, I'm your candidate. If Shearson isn't seeking these qualities in their employees, then perhaps you're right. Perhaps I'm not what you're looking for."

The interviewer, who closes every interview with the "I don't think you're what we're looking for" line, liked Alan because he overcame an objection with self-confidence and poise. He didn't take no for an answer. Shearson seeks leaders—not complacent followers.

I routinely interview college graduates for sales representative positions. The more specific applicants are about what they've done and about how those experiences have affected them, the more I'm convinced they'd be valuable employees. It's not enough just to say what you've done; you have to demonstrate that you've thought about how each of your experiences has contributed to your personal or professional development.

I recently interviewed two applicants. The first had all the right "canned" responses. He had obviously prepared for the interview by reading one of the books on interviewing, but he hadn't prepared by thinking through his thoughts so that his responses would be distinguishable from those of the other applicants. He just didn't stand out from the crowd. He did not exude interest, enthusiasm or confidence.

Toward the end of the interview, I gave him another chance to show some initiative: I gave him my business card and told him to call me if he had any questions about the position or about career opportunities within the company. Perhaps he could have redeemed himself if he had called later with specific questions. He could have written a follow-up note. I never heard from him again. Despite his high grades and his work experience, we didn't call him back either. Thanks, but no, thanks . . .

I was skeptical of the second applicant because he was a preppie Yale grad. (I'm not a preppie or a Yale grad.)

This was an outrageous prejudice, I realize. But it's a good example of a mind-set you will undoubtedly encounter—in one form or another—and have to bulldoze past with confidence, preparedness and authenticity. I asked Ted some of the usual questions. He responded with enthusiasm, imagination and humor. He didn't strike me as someone bored by the possibility of work. (There goes that prejudice again.) He'd played intramural sports, was involved as a class officer, had a summer internship in clinical psychology in the Bronx and, for two years, was a Big Brother. And he had high aspirations. He asked all about career track opportunities and my own career path within the company, and outlined the future he envisioned for himself. Within the first five minutes this applicant sent my preconceptions right out the window.

I asked him what some of his lifelong career goals were. He said, "I want to go into politics in the second half of my career. I want to be President."

We hired him. His determination, his track record and his belief in his own ability to go forward made him a winner in my book. He'll succeed because he believes he can. By the way, if he does run for President at some point, he's got a campaign manager in me.

Back to the prejudice for a moment. Perhaps you'll have to overcome a prejudice someone may have about the school you did or did not attend or the activity you did or did not join. Make that you *will*, one of these days, have to overcome some kind of prejudice to get a job. Relax. So does everybody else. There were interviewers who were undoubtedly unimpressed because I had *not* gone to Oxford on a Fulbright, followed by two years in Ethiopia with the Peace Corps, capped by a year in Paris at the Cordon Bleu Culinary Institute before my return Stateside to pursue a career in marketing.

The trick is to be yourself. Give it your best shot, be direct and be professional. (Come on . . . if they want to make you company president, it won't take more than two hours of professionalism on your part. Think big picture.) Identifying and overcoming objections—and bad attitudes—is part of being a pro at the interviewing process. It's also part of being a successful team player once you're hired.

Your Interview

You've marketed yourself with your résumé and cover letter. Now comes the big sell. You'll need to chronicle your experience so that your interviewer knows you're prepared for the job. Rehearse for confidence. And follow up after the interview—absolutely.

Before the interview:

1. **RESEARCH.** Check out the company and the job. The better prepared you are for the interview, the more confidence you will project. Talk to people who work at the company or who hold similar positions for rival firms. Go to the library and research the company. Look in Standard & Poor's Register of Corporations or Moody's Manual. Check *Forbes*, *Fortune* or other business magazines.

   Know the company's history and current climate. This is the type of knowledge that helps people at both ends of the interviewing seesaw. Not only will it impress your interviewer; it will also help you decide if the company interests you. Develop questions about the company and the job.

2. **REHEARSE.** Before your interview, rehearse answers to questions likely to be asked. Ask friends to play interviewer and give them a list of questions to ask you. If you do not have someone to help you role-play, practice by yourself. Become comfortable and confident about your accomplishments. Without sounding arrogant, you want the interviewer to know that you are ambitious and self-assured.

   You may want to interview with a few companies in which you're not particularly interested just to get the experience of the interview before you talk to recruiters from the companies at the top of your wish list. Keep an open mind. The company you are least interested in initially could be the one that impresses you the most. Even after you've asked a friend to simulate an actual interview, continue to think and brainstorm the really tough questions you're likely to be asked. If you communicate effectively, your interviewer will be convinced of your abilities beyond your "paper" credentials.

3. **RELAX.** If you've followed the first two steps, you have every reason to be confident as you walk into the interviewer's office. So relax, be yourself and enjoy the experience. If worse comes to worst, try to manage at least the first two-thirds of this formula.

4. **DRESS FOR SUCCESS.** This may seem trivial, but it is important to those who are interviewing you. Your appearance says a lot about you, so invest in one good interviewing suit and shirt. Look neat, alert and enthusiastic. Again, you're promoting yourself, so you want to exude the best "you" possible. Don't take any shortcuts.

Now for a few tips from combat veterans. "Let the interviewer set the pace," advises Steve Kendall, a recruiter for Nabisco. "The biggest turnoff in job interviews are pat answers riddled with anxiety and interviewees who control the interview too abrasively in the first part of the conversation. Use the time in the last quarter of the interview to ask questions and gather information about the company."

Steve appreciates interviewees who are animated, sincere and forthright. "I want to see the applicant use examples to convince me of his or her qualifications and potential for success."

Common Interview Questions

When Steve Kendall conducts an interview, two of his favorite questions are: "Why are you interested in working for my company?" and "What are some examples of how you persuaded others to your way of thinking?" (How would you respond right now to those two questions?)

Here are some of the most common questions interviewers ask college graduates. Use the sample answers as a starting point for figuring out answers of your own.

1. "Why should we hire you?"

(Worst possible response: "Because.")

This is a springboard from which to list the qualities that will make you a great employee. Be brief in your descriptions and use specific examples to illustrate your points:

"I'm conscientious, tireless and committed to going above and beyond what is expected of me. Last summer, as an intern with the New York Stock Exchange, I was always the first in to work and the last to leave at night. I made several excellent contacts, including the president of Merrill Lynch, who offered me a part-time job during the school year."

2. "Tell me about your education."

"It's over."

Wrong, wrong! This question is meant to find out how much emphasis you've put on your academic education. If you've made good or great grades, terrific. If not, explain why—you worked twenty-five hours a week, completely supported yourself and your foster family of five, took eighteen units each semester, got your pilot's license, etc. If you've learned a lot from taking the top-flight, more rigorous professors, say so, but only if it's true. Never fudge in an interview. In addition to being unethical, the fact that you are padding your own story is painfully obvious to people who recruit for a living.

"Although my GPA is 3.2, I've made 4.0 for the last two academic years. I took serious classes, looked to my professors as mentors and truly challenged myself. I'm proud of what I've learned during college."

3. "Tell me something about yourself."

(Stifle the following: "Taurus, Cancer Rising, Moon in Sagittarius.")

Like the first question, this is an open-ended query in which the interviewer wants specifics on who you are. Are you an achiever? Are you detail-oriented? Are you reliable? Are you a fast learner? Are you good at balancing several things at once? Would you have a cool head in a hot situation? What about the personal side of you? How are you perceived by others? Are you frequently available to help? Are you patient?

"I'm an enthusiastic, determined and highly self-motivated person. I take a great deal of pride in being successful in work and play. I've tried hard to develop my outside interests, some of which my friends and family consider crazy. I like to sky-dive, spelunk (crawl around in caves) and read science fiction. I also love organizing big groups of people—for outdoor concerts, the annual summer renaissance festival, canoeing trips, etc. My greatest weakness is that I have so many interests that I tend to take on too much at times."

By analyzing these responses, you can see how you must "think on your feet" to answer questions in positive, concrete and self-affirming ways. But the more questions you know now and the more responses you've thought through and rehearsed, the better you'll be able to "close" your interview.

Here is an additional list of frequently asked questions for you to think about and rehearse. (You'll notice that some of these questions are similar to those in Chapter 2 on defining who you are. Compare the answers from your freshman year with the answers to your interview questions. How have you changed?)

1. Tell me about a specific goal you have set and achieved—at school or at work.

2. How much drive do you have? Describe a typical day and week.

3. What kind of experience do you have for this job?

4. Where do you see yourself five years from now?

5. Where do you see yourself ten years from now?

6. What was your greatest defeat and how did you overcome it?

7. What is your greatest accomplishment?

8. What do you do in your spare time?

9. Who are your heroes? Why are they your heroes?

10. What book has had the greatest impact on you?

11. What interests you most about this job?

12. How would a previous employer or professor describe you?

13. How would your friends describe you?

14. At the end of your life, what would you like people to say about you?

15. Why company X?

How You Will Be Evaluated

There are a number of different categories in which your interviewer will evaluate you. On a scale of 1 to 5, 1 being the lowest, rate yourself in the following areas (use one or more *specific* examples):

Problem Solving and Priority Setting

Would you be able to understand and take action to solve even the most complex and difficult problems?

Achieving Goals

Would you consistently set and achieve goals? Are you results-oriented?

Motivating Others

Would you be effective at getting others to see your point of view? Could you motivate even your less enthusiastic co-workers?

Working Well with Others

Would you work well with and gain the respect of your co-workers?

Responsibility

Would you keep your word and be responsible to co-workers and clients?

Tenacity

Would you be determined to work well through even the most mundane parts of the job?

Detail-Oriented

Would you pay attention to even the smallest details while keeping the larger goals in focus?

Vision

Do you envision a mission? Do you look beyond the game and see all the way to the championship?

Resilience

Do you bounce back from defeat? Do you treat setbacks as stepping-stones? Do you, despite the difficult nature of a situation, explore other avenues? Do you consistently test new ideas?

Other Criteria

Every interviewer has his or her own criteria for evaluating you. Many of the Fortune 500 companies judge prospective employees in six categories for entry-level positions: (1) Achieving Goals, (2) Influencing Others, (3) Problem Solving and Priority Setting, (4) Developing Cooperative Relations, (5) Responsiveness in Contacts with Others and (6) Working Well with Facts and Figures. Employers also look for talent and potential, so convince them that you'll be worth their investment in both the short and the long run.

Basically, most companies will evaluate you as Excellent, Good, Fair or Weak on four points. They are:

1. Personal: How do you come across? Are you strongly motivated or sluggish? Are you energetic or lazy? Do you have long-term

goals or are you aimless? Are you articulate or shy? Friendly or boorish?

2. Professional: Are you reliable? Are you honest? Can you inspire others? Are you able to juggle a number of projects at once? Are you decisive? Do you follow through?

3. Accomplishments: Can you describe your proudest achievements? What have they taught you? How have you grown from the challenges you've faced?

4. Potential: Do you think long-term? Do you place a high value on continuing your education and building new skills? Will you be a good investment for the company? Do you show signs of long-term interest in the industry or will you be off to business or law school in one year?

Your college placement office is likely to have several books and videos on how to research companies and how to interview effectively. The placement office will also have a lot of information on companies that interview on campus. Most companies will give the placement office large notebooks describing the history of the company and various positions available. You can only make sure it will be a good match for you if you have sufficient information. Get it. It will allow you to be savvy and well informed in your interview.

Rejection

You'll have to deal with rejection during the interviewing process. Keep a positive attitude and remember that you will find a job. Commit yourself to that end. Believe in your capabilities and overcome all objections.

It was hard for Chris Nelson, who majored in economics. After graduate school he searched for three years for a good banking job. He kept his head up, realizing that the "perfect job was just around the corner." Finally he landed a job with First Boston. If you are talented and work hard, he says, the only other quality you'll need is perseverance.

Epilogue

No matter how the interview goes, be sure to send a thank-you note. You never can tell. Better safe than sorry.

·12·

YOU'RE HIRED!
Landing the Job

The true objective is to take chaos as given and learn to thrive on it.
TOM PETERS, *Thriving on Chaos*

One must be something to be able to do something.
GOETHE

You did not laugh uncontrollably during any of your interviews, unless specifically requested to do so. You did not misplace your identity; you were confident and authentic. You looked professional and poised. We're talking home run.

Now come a few very important details. After each interview, write a thank-you note and then wait two weeks. If you haven't heard from the company, call the interviewer to see if you're still under consideration. If so, could you make an appointment to see them again? This is an important follow-up gesture. Persistence pays.

Do They Want You?

At this point you'll have some indication of whether you're in or out. If you're still in, one or more of the following could happen:

1. You spend a day in the office or in the field to get a feeling for the job firsthand. If the interviewer doesn't propose this, request it. It could mean the difference between a job you love and a job you hate.

2. You're invited to a dinner or lunch so the prospective employer may observe you in a social setting. Are you friendly or abrasive? Are you well mannered or boorish? Do you spill your drink on the white divan or your future boss? Do you listen to others or

165

dominate conversations? Be sure to exhibit your star qualities of enthusiasm and poise.

3. You could meet again with the interviewer. In this case, press them to introduce you to other employees. Don't count on the recruiter alone to provide you with a comprehensive picture of the company.

4. You're flown to the home office. This is optimal since it's in your best interest to know the philosophy and daily workings of the company. You will be introduced to lots of different people. Hold fast to your energy! You need to be as sharp and enthusiastic in your final interview as in your first. You can wilt after it's all over!

5. You take a series of tests—analytical, verbal, logic, etc., during your continued interview.

These steps vary from company to company. The bottom line is: be poised, inquisitive and attentive. Act as though you want the job— even if you haven't decided. After each interview, send an additional follow-up letter.

Do You Want Them?

After your second interview and talks with your "contacts," decide if the job is right for you. If it's your only job offer, you may have to take it. That's okay. You may discover you like the job. If not, there's nothing to stop you from seeking out other positions.

Find out:

1. Starting salary _____

2. Bonus _____

3. Company car _____

4. Travel? If so, how much? _____

5. What are the projected timetables for promotion? _____

_____

6. What are the "career track" positions? _____

_____

7. Does the benefit program include medical and dental plans?

_____

8. Is there a profit-sharing program? _____ _____

9. Is there a retirement plan? _____

10. Is there a tuition reimbursement program? _____

11. Do they cover travel and moving expenses? _____

12. What kind of formal training will you receive? _____

_____

13. When could you start? _____ _____

If you have several job offers, list the pros and cons of the company in which you're most interested. Here's an example:

Prospective Company Evaluation Sheet

PROS	CONS
Company car	Relocation
Bonus and salary	Too much travel???
Interesting job	Office in home
Growth potential	Solitary job
Fortune 500 company	No formal training program for
Great co-workers (How do you know?)	six months
Excellent product	

Prospective Company Evaluation Sheet

PROS	CONS
1.	

2.

3.

4.

5.

6.

7.

8.

9.

10.

People I've Met

NAME	DATE	COMMENTS
1.		
2.		
3.		

4.

5.

6.

7.

8.

9.

10.

Getting the Offer

On your follow-up interview, bring up salary ranges and benefits. If the recruiter starts shuffling piles of paper on top of the desk and skirting the issue, don't be deterred. Return to the point later, as you sum up. You need to know about salary in order to make your decision. No employer will be insulted by your pursuing this line of questioning. In fact, they'll probably respect you for it.

After you have all of the answers to these questions and any others that pop into your head, ask your interviewers if they have any more questions for you. If they do, answer them. If not, state that, on the basis of what you've heard and all the information you've gathered, you would very much like to work for them. Personalize your closing conversation. Tell them what has impressed you about their company and be specific. Recount examples of the past few weeks or months which have led you to your conclusion. Then ask plainly when you can expect to receive a job offer.

When you close your interview, the interviewer may ask if you've interviewed with any other firms. Be honest. But be on your guard.

Even if you're not interested in the other companies, don't let them know that. You want to hold on to your bargaining power. If they think they're the only company you are interested in or that is interested in you, they may make you a low offer.

If you're offered the position on the spot, *don't* accept. Tell them you need some time to think it over but make a commitment to call back with your answer. Then review your list of pros and cons with your mentors from college jobs, professors, friends and parents.

Negotiating Salary

"When I accepted my first job out of college with the accounting firm of Touche Ross, I had two other offers from well-respected firms," says Donald Mason, who now works in Dallas for a private firm. "Because Touche Ross knew I was attractive to several employers, they offered me more money to start than the typical college grad."

In your first job out of college, you don't have tremendous bargaining power but you might have some. Use it.

Employers never offer their highest or even their middle-range salary. They start low because they expect to negotiate with you. Push for a higher salary. Point out:

1. You're more experienced than most people who have been out of college for two or three years because you gained four years of real-world experience during college. You're much more qualified and promising than the average college grad.
2. State what other people make in similar jobs within the same industry.
3. State any higher offers you've received to see if they'll increase theirs.

Don't push so hard that you alienate your new boss. But if you get $2,000 over the initial offer, terrific. If you haven't done anything in college to prove that you are better qualified than the pack of applicants, take what you're offered. You can prove yourself on the job and poise yourself for the best raises.

Accepting

Do it gracefully. After you've ironed out the salary issue, accept the offer with a positive, reaffirming statement. Some companies require a formal letter of acceptance.

This is your first official chance to "bond" with your new manager.

You may want to take the initiative at the outset and ask about goals for your first year on the job. What defines minimum requirements? What exceeds requirements? What do you have to do to be outstanding in your first year? Together, you may want to put some specific goals on paper so that you have something to refer to throughout the year. At salary-review time, you will have something concrete with which to gauge your work, a contract of sorts between you and your manager.

Tying Up Loose Ends

Write thank-you letters to the companies you turned down. Thank them for their time. You may want to call those who gave you special attention. Leave all doors open for the future.

You might also write thank-you notes to those who turned you down. You'll probably be qualified to work for them in the future. Maintain a favorable impression in their minds.

Starting

When should you start? That depends on how you're planning to celebrate finishing college. If you've been waiting to backpack through Indonesia with your suite mates and have slept with a map of the South Seas above your pillow for three years running, don't forsake this for a briefcase and a suit. The briefcase will be there when you get back, and student loans don't come due for nine months following graduation. Take the time while you've got it. If, on the other hand, you can't wait to close in on that corner office, go for it. The job is yours. You can still see the world in two-week intervals during your summer vacations.

Other Incidentals

You'll have to fill out insurance and benefit forms. You may also have some "soft" or formal training. Even if you are hurried right into your job with the minimum of instruction, don't worry. Ask questions. Solicit advice. Work hard. Learn all you can.

Starting your new job may scare you as much as starting college. Be patient. Your period of adjustment will be easier and shorter than that of your peers who are less prepared for the real world. Keep using all the techniques you learned in your internships and other jobs. Within about six months, you should feel like an ace who's been with the company for years.

·13·

OUTLOOKS AND INSIGHTS
Succeeding on the Job and in Life

It is as though I had lost my way and asked someone the way home. He says he will show me and walks with me along a smoother path which suddenly stops. And now my friend tells me: "All you have to do is find your way home from here."
LUDWIG WITTGENSTEIN, *Culture and Value*

In order that people may be happy in their work, these three things are needed: They must be fit for it. They must not do too much of it. And they must have a sense of success in it.
JOHN RUSKIN

No matter what your first job after college happens to be, it is a first step. But it is also a point of departure. If you started with the company and the position of your dreams, great. Your job might also be less than terrific. But you have to start somewhere, building your skills, meeting people and developing work habits. That's a positive, exciting challenge.

You'll go from there to a string of promotions, to a better job with another company, to a smaller company, back to graduate school or to begin your own company. Your first job is like a blank page. You fill it in as you go. And your options are limitless as long as you pursue them.

Games People Play

In the real world, people measure themselves by all kinds of things—how much money they make, what their job is, how many people they

173

know, how many dates they have, what kind of clothes they wear or what kind of car they drive.

Many of these things have to do with *appearances*, not reality. They reflect what people want others to think, not necessarily what they really are. Know the difference between the two and be true to yourself and your values. The best job in the world isn't worth much if you are not happy. Similarly, no amount of money or possessions you can buy will satisfy you if you aren't content with who *you* are.

This book is about defining those things which are important to *you*, and you alone. So resist comparing yourself with those around you. That's a game you'll never win. There will always be people who are better and worse off than you. In college and in life, it's important to do what you believe and what you feel is right.

People may not always agree with you, especially if they feel threatened by your abilities. That's okay. Preserve your integrity and don't let someone get the better of you. Your satisfaction will come from knowing that you took the high road.

President John F. Kennedy said it best in his inaugural address:

> For of those to whom much is given, much is required. And when at some future date the high court of history sits in judgment on each of us, recording whether in our brief span of service we fulfilled our responsibilities to the state, our success or failure, in whatever office we hold, will be measured by four questions: First, were we truly men of courage . . . Second, were we truly men of judgment . . . Third, were we truly men of integrity . . . Finally, were we truly men of dedication?

Is It Ethical?

Ask yourself these questions: Would others approve of my behavior if they knew about it? Would I want someone else to behave similarly? Is what I'm doing right for the company? Is what the company is doing right? If not, how do I handle it? What are my own personal standards and how do I define them?

In journalism, the accepted rule for quotes is that if someone says something to you and then says, "Don't print that," only *after* he made the statement, you are allowed to print it. But several journalists I've talked to said they would not print the quote if it was made by a "civilian," a nonpolitician or anyone not familiar with the rules of the press. The reason? Plain fairness.

On Being Happy

Once you've landed your job, take pride in what you do. Concentrate not just on job success but on overall happiness. If there is any one point which this book makes, it's the importance of balancing several goals—personal and professional. Your job is only one aspect of your life.

It takes a strong commitment and hard work to maintain a healthy balance on the job and off. Being happy won't just happen. Like anything else, you have to work at it.

In a graduation speech to students at his alma mater, MIT, Kenneth Olsen, CEO of Digital Equipment Corporation, reflected on his thirty years of work since graduating from college: "Running a business is not the important thing. Making a commitment to do a good job, to improve things, to influence the world is where it's at. I would also suggest that one of the most satisfying things is to help others to be creative and take responsibility. These are the important things."

"Your most precious commodity is not material," says Charles S. Sanford, Jr., CEO of Bankers Trust New York Corporation. "It is and always will be your time." If you keep work in balance with other things in your life, Sanford says, you can accomplish even more on the job. "Read a little poetry, enjoy friends, and most of all, don't take yourself too seriously. In the final analysis, whatever you have accomplished won't be worth much unless you've had fun."

Okay, so the cynic in you cries: How much time did these CEOs spend working in their twenties and thirties? Good point. They probably spent a lot of time, but you have to ask yourself: Do you want to be a CEO? Most people would say, "No, thanks." You have to carefully weigh the trade-offs of your long-term goals against what you are doing—and enjoying—in the short term. The majority of the population thrive quite happily between entry-level positions and the top of the heap. They enjoy their work and still have the time to be with their friends and raise a family.

Maybe you won't have all the money in the world, but you will have had time to enjoy those things which count the most when you're ninety—a job you liked, a lifestyle you enjoyed and the opportunity to contribute to your own growth and that of others.

Thoughts for the Journey

I began this book with a personal anecdote, so I'd like to end with one. It has to do with becoming discouraged. And it is a story without which this book truly would have no closure.

About three months before I finished this manuscript, I was exhausted. My job was quite tedious—not because the work itself had changed, but because my approach to it had. I made little time to see my friends, and at night I just wanted to go to sleep early. Boring. In short, I was doing all those things I have said throughout the book never to do. Realizing that I wasn't being myself, and knowing for a fact that I wasn't having a good time, I decided to take a break to get back the perspective I knew was missing.

Egypt was the place for perspective. Why Egypt? It was exotic, distant and vastly different from life as I knew it. Moreover, one of my interests is travel, and after my junior year in Spain, I made a personal promise to visit as many countries as I could. So off I went for the first time on a vacation by myself, leaving my "normal" life and my work behind me.

When I saw the pyramids at dusk, a renewed energy and inspiration filled me. The 4,500-year-old pyramids symbolize balance, perfection, human achievement and teamwork. (Fortunately, today we can work in teams in business and organizations; the Egyptians dictated to slaves in the most oppressive style.) Witnessing the achievements of an ancient culture that survived 4,500 years left me with a feeling of great awe and real humility. I wondered how many American monuments would survive 450 years, let alone into the year 6500.

Clearly, the Egyptians saw no limits to what they could accomplish. They saw things not in terms of what they were in the moment, but in terms of what they could become in time. They made dreams into realities.

Well, bully for Tut, you say, but what has this got to do with college and careers and human potential? The pyramids helped me to recover my "edge," my own potential. The tensions loosened inside of me and confidence took over.

My perspective restored, I was free to concentrate on challenges, including work, the book and my personal life, with confidence and energy.

Throughout your life, the inspirations that motivate you will ebb and flow. You won't always feel inspired and you won't always perform at peak. The important thing to remember when you reach an impasse is not to panic. Remove yourself from the ordinary—through reading *Don*

Quixote or going to a concert or exhibit or taking a day trip by yourself. Maybe your most relaxing time is spent watching a football game or a weekly sitcom. That's fine. Just allow yourself time to unwind and replenish your own central energy source.

The Blue Sky Ahead

You have a lot to be proud of. If you are reading this book for the first time as a freshman, you get credit for getting this far, and for committing yourself to making college and your career pursuit everything they can be. Good for you.

If you are looking at this chapter for the last time, and you have a job and you're wondering how four years could come and go so fast, take time to pat yourself on the back. Look down from where you are now, realize how far you've come and be proud of your accomplishments. The next peak you scale, your first job, is very similar to what you've learned in the last few years. Accept the challenges that are before you. And in addition to doing a good or a great job, give to the world something of what it has given to you through your family, your friends, your activities and your actions. Don't be typical. You are unique. Show the world the special gifts and contributions which only you have to offer.

And so here's to your unique success story. Here's to the ability which you have to dream the dream and make it real. Go change the world. Goodbye and good luck.

APPENDICES

APPENDICES

Appendix 1

Companies with Summer/ Winter Internships

Below is a directory of summer internships from Betsy Bauer's book *Getting Work Experience*. (In it you'll find full descriptions of each job, qualifications needed and salary, if any.) These are only some of the summer internships available across the country. There are thousands of others—summer, winter and semester-long—for college students. Don't forget to propose your own summer internships at one of the local businesses in your home or university town.

Advertising/Public Relations

Abramson Associates, Inc.
1275 K Street N.W.
Washington, D.C. 20005
(202) 289-6900

John Adams Associates, Inc.
1825 K Street N.W.
Washington, D.C. 20006
(202) 466-8320

American Association of Advertising Agencies, Inc.
666 Third Avenue
New York, NY 10017
(212) 682-2500

Burson-Marsteller, Inc.
230 Park Avenue South
New York, NY 10010
(212) 614-4000

Dow Jones & Company
22 Cortlandt Street
New York, NY 10007
(212) 285-5000

Ruder Finn & Rotman, Inc.
110 E. 59th Street
New York, NY 10022
(212) 593-6400

Business/Industry

A & M Records
1416 North La Brea Avenue
Hollywood, CA 90028
(213) 469-2411

Advanced Micro Devices
901 Thompson Place
Box 3453
Sunnyvale, CA 94088
(408) 749-3130

Aetna Life and Casualty Company
Corporate Recruiting
Office DA09
151 Farmington Avenue
Hartford, CN 06156
(203) 273-0123

Air Products and Chemical, Inc.
Box 538
Allentown, PA 18105
(215) 481-4911

Allied Corporation
P.O. Box 2245R
Morristown, NJ 07960
(201) 455-2000

Allstate Insurance Companies
Allstate Plaza S. G1C
Northbrook, IL 60062
(312) 291-5000

Amdahl Corporation
1250 East Arques Avenue
Sunnyvale, CA 94086
(408) 746-6000

American Cyanamid Co.
One Cyanamid Plaza
Wayne, NJ 07470
(201) 831-2000

American International Group
72 Wall Street
New York, NY 10270
(212) 770-6812

Ashland Oil, Inc.
P.O. Box 391
Ashland, KY 41101
(606) 329-3333

Ball Corporation
345 South High Street
Muncie, IN 47302
(317) 747-6127

Bank of Boston
P.O. Box 1976
Boston, MA 02105
(617) 542-2472

Bank of New York
48 Wall Street
21st Floor
New York, NY 10015
(212) 530-8609

BDM Corporation
7915 Jones Branch Drive
McLean, VA 22102
(703) 927-7571

Beatrice Companies
Corporate Offices
2 North La Salle Street
Chicago, IL 60602
(312) 782-3820

Boston Edison Company
800 Boylston Street
Boston, MA 02199
(617) 424-2000

Brown Forman Distillers Corporation
Box 1080
Louisville, KY 40201
(502) 585-1100

Burger King Corporation
Box 520783
General Mail Facility
Miami, FL 33152
(305) 596-7011

Burlington Northern Railroad
3000 Continental Plaza
777 Main Street
Fort Worth, TX 76102
(817) 878-3031

Campbell Soup Company
Campbell Place
Camden, NJ 08101
(609) 342-4800

Carolina Power and Light
P.O. Box 1551
Raleigh, NC 27602
(919) 836-6111

CBT Corporation
99 Founders Plaza
East Hartford, CN 06108
(203) 244-5000

Central Bancorp, Inc.
5th and Main Streets
Cincinnati, OH 45202
(513) 651-8915

Centran Corporation
800 Superior Avenue
Cleveland, OH 44114
(216) 687-1200

Chrysler Corporation
Box 1919
Detroit, MI 48288
(313) 956-5252

Cigna Corporation
A-139
Hartford, CN 06152
(203) 726-6000

Control Data Corporation
P.O. Box O
Minneapolis, MN 55440
(612) 853-5035

Cray Research, Inc.
Software Development Division
1440 Northland Drive
Menota Heights, MN 55120
(612) 333-5889

Dataproducts Corporation
6200 Canoga Avenue
Woodland Hills, CA 91365
(818) 887-8000

Digital Equipment Corporation
146 Main Street
Maynard, MA 01754
(617) 897-5111

Eaton Corporation
AIL Division
Commack Road
Deer Park, NY 11729
(516) 595-5000

Export-Import Bank of the
United States
811 Vermont Avenue NW
Washington, D.C. 20571
(202) 566-8990

Fairchild Industries, Inc.
20301 Century Boulevard
Germantown, MD 20874
(301) 428-6000

Federal Home Loan Mortgage
Corporation
1776 G Street N.W.
P.O. Box 37248
Washington, D.C. 20013
(202) 789-4700

Federal Mogul Corporation
P.O. Box 1966
Detroit, MI 48235
(313) 354-7700

Financial Women's Association of
New York
1221 Avenue of the Americas
New York, NY 10020
(212) 764-6476

First Atlanta Corporation
2400 Piedmanon Road
Atlanta, GA 30324
(404) 588-5000

First National Bank of Chicago
1 First National Plaza
Chicago, IL 60670
(312) 732-4000

First Wisconsin Corporation
777 East Wisconsin
Milwaukee, WI 53202
(414) 765-4985

Flow General, Inc.
7655 Old Springhouse Road
McLean, VA 22102
(703) 893-5915

Fort Howard Paper Company
1919 South Broadway
Green Bay, WI 54304
(414) 435-8821

Freeman Chemical Corporation
222 East Main Street
Port Washington, WI 53074
(414) 284-5541

Frito Lay, Inc.
Box 35034
Dallas, TX 75235
(214) 351-7000

Genentech, Inc.
460 Point San Bruno Boulevard
San Francisco, CA 94080
(415) 266-1000

General Motors Corporation
Central Office
3044 West Grand Boulevard
Detroit, MI 48202
(313) 556-5000

Georgia-Pacific Corporation
133 Peachtree Street, N.E.
Atlanta, GA 30303
(404) 521-4000

W. R. Grace & Company
Grace Plaza
1114 Avenue of the Americas
New York, NY 10036
(212) 819-6309

GTE Corporation
One Stamford Forum
Stamford, CN 06901
(203) 965-3961

Hallmark Cards
P.O. Box 580
Kansas City, MO 64141
(816) 274-4062

Hercules, Inc.
Hercules Plaza
Wilmington, DE 19894
(302) 594-5000

Hewlett-Packard Company
3000 Hanover Street
Palo Alto, CA 94304
(415) 857-1501

Hoffman-La Roche, Inc.
340 Kingsland Street
Nutley, NJ 07110
(201) 235-4738

Honeywell, Inc.
Honeywell Plaza
Minneapolis, MN 55408
(612) 870-2160

Hughes Aircraft Company
200 North Sepulveda
El Segundo, CA 90245
(213) 305-4149

Indiana Bell Telephone Company,
Inc.
220 North Meridian Street
Indianapolis, IN 46204
(317) 265-3617

Inroads, Inc.
1221 Locust, Suite 755
St. Louis, MO 63103
(314) 241-7330

International Foundation for
Employee Benefit Plans
18700 West Bluemound Road
P.O. Box 69
Brookfield, WI 53005
(414) 786-6700

International Paper Company
77 West 45th Street
New York, NY 10036
(212) 536-6249

Kellogg Company
235 Porter Street
Battle Creek, MI 49016
(616) 966-2405

Kohler Company
Kohler, WI 53044
(414) 457-4441

Litton Microwave Cooking Products
Litton Industries, Inc.
1405 Xenium Lane North
Minneapolis, MN 55440
(612) 553-2210

LTV Corporation
P.O. Box 225907
Dallas, TX 75265
(212) 266-4600

Marine Midland Banks
One Marine Midland Center
Buffalo, NY 14240
(716) 843-2424

McDonnell Douglas
Astronautics Company
McDonnell Douglas Corporation
5301 Bolsa Avenue
Huntington Beach, CA 92647
(714) 896-3311

Mead Johnson & Company
2404 Pennsylvania Street
Evansville, IN 47721
(812) 426-6000

Medtronics, Inc.
Box 1453
Minneapolis, MN 55440
(612) 574-4000

Merck & Company, Inc.
Box 2000
Rahway, NJ 07065
(201) 574-4000

Michigan Bell Telephone Company
444 Michigan Avenue
Detroit, MI 48226
(313) 223-8177

Minnesota Mining and
Manufacturing Company
3M Center
St. Paul, MN 55144
(612) 733-1035

Motorola, Inc.
1303 Algonquin Road
Schaumburg, IL 60196
(312) 397-5000

Nabisco Brands, Inc.
7 Campus Drive
Parsippany, NJ 07054
(201) 884-4000

NCR Corporation
Dayton, OH 45479
(513) 445-5000

New York City Summer
Management Intern Program
Department of Personnel
220 Church Street, Room 338
New York, NY 10013

Norton Company
1 New Bond Street
Worcester, MA 01606
(508) 795-5000

Oscar Mayer & Company, Inc.
910 Mayer Avenue
Madison, WI 53707
(608) 241-3311

Owens-Corning Fiberglas
Corporation
Fiberglas Tower
Toledo, OH 43659
(419) 248-8281

Perkin-Elmer Corporation
Main Avenue
Norwalk, CO 06856
(203) 762-1000

Philadelphia Electric Company
2301 Market Street
P.O. Box 8699
Philadelphia, PA 19101
(215) 841-4340

Philip Morris USA
P.O. Box 26603
Richmond, VA 23261
(804) 274-3640

Pillsbury Company
Pillsbury Center
Minneapolis, MN 55402
(612) 330-4769

Provident Life & Accident Insurance
Company
Fountain Square
Chattanooga, TN 37402
(615) 755-1246

Public Relations Student Society of
America
845 Third Avenue
New York, NY 10022
(212) 826-1774

Public Service Company of Colorado
P.O. Box 840
Denver, CO 80201
(303) 571-7511

Quantum Corporation
Milpitas, CA 95035
(408) 262-1100

Rockwell International
2230 East Imperial Highway
El Segundo, CA 90245
(213) 594-2495

Savin Corporation,
Technology Operations
P.O. Box 4500
Binghamton, NY 13902
(607) 722-5012

Shared Medical System, Inc.
51 Valley Stream Parkway
Malvern, PA 19355
(215) 296-6300

Standard Oil Company of Indiana
200 East Randolph Drive
Chicago, IL 60601
(312) 856-6111

Steelcase, Inc.
P.O. Box 1967
Grand Rapids, MI 49508
(616) 246-9332

Tektronix, Inc.
12901 S.W. Jenkins Road
Beaverton, OR 97077
(503) 627-8130

Transamerica Occidental Life
Insurance Company
1150 South Olive, Suite 519-T
Los Angeles, CA 90015
(213) 742-3435

Twin City Area Urban Corps
107B City Hall
Minneapolis, MN 55415
(612) 348-6967

Union Carbide Corporation
Old Ridgebury Road
Danbury, CN 06817
(203) 794-6526

United States General Accounting
Office
441 G Street N.W., Room 4650
Washington, D.C. 20548
(202) 275-6092

Criminal Justice & Education

Association of Student International
Law Societies
2223 Massachusetts Avenue N.W.
Washington, D.C. 20008
(202) 387-8467

Colorado Outdoor Education Center
for the Handicapped
P.O. Box 697
Brenkenridge, CO 80424
(303) 453-6422

Connecticut Department of Adult
Probation
643 Maple Avenue
Hartford, CN 06114
(203) 566-8350

Council for Advancement and Support of Education
11 Dupont Circle, Suite 400
Washington, D.C. 20036
(202) 328-5900

Elwyn Institutes
111 Elwyn Road
Elwyn, PA 19063
(215) 358-6592

Hinton Rural Life Center
P.O. Box 27
Hayesville, NC 28904
(704) 389-8336

Interlocken Center for Experiential
Education
RFD 2, Box 165
Hillsboro, NH 03244
(603) 478-3202

The Marion County Wilderness
Challenge Program
3030 Center Street NE
Salem, OR 97301
(503) 588-5324

National 4-H Club Foundation
7100 Connecticut Avenue
Chevy Chase, MD 20015
(301) 656-9000

Northern California Service League
1104 Harrison Street
San Francisco, CA 94103
(415) 863-2323

Northfield Mount Hermon School
Northfield, MA 01360
(413) 498-5311

St. Paul's School
Advanced Studies Program
Concord, NH 03301
(603) 225-3341

Sunrise Lake Outdoor Education
Center/Northwest Suburban Special
Education Organization
7N749 Route 59
Bartlett, IL 60103
(312) 830-0146

United States Supreme Court Judicial
Internship Program
Office of Administrative Assistant
Washington, D.C. 20543
(202) 252-3400

Environment

The Arnold Arboretum of
Harvard University
The Arborway
Jamaica Plain, MA 02130
(617) 524-1718

Atlantic Center for the Environment
39 South Main Street
Ipswich, MA 011938-2321
(617) 356-0038

Aullwood Audubon Center and
Farm
100 Aullwood Road
Dayton, OH 45414
(513) 890-7360

Bradford Woods Outdoor Education,
Recreation, and Camping Center
5040 State Road 67 North
Martinsville, IN 46151
(812) 335-0227

The Chattanooga Nature Center at
Reflection Riding
Route 4
Garden Road
Chattanooga, TN 37409
(615) 821-1160

The Environmental Learning Center,
Inc.
Star Route Box 191A
Isabella, MN 55607
(218) 323-7733

Fairfax County Park Authority
4030 Hummer Road
Annandale, VA 22003
(703) 941-5000

International Crane Foundation
Route 1 Box 230C
Shady Lane Road
Baraboo, WI 53913
(608) 356-9462

Laughing Brook Education Center
and Wildlife Sanctuary
Massachusetts Audubon Society
789 Main Street
Hampden, MA 01036
(413) 566-8034

Longwood Gardens, Inc.
Kennett Square, PA 19348-1000
(215) 388-6741

Minnesota Zoo
Apple Valley, MN 55124
(612) 432-9010

Morton Arboretum
Lisle, IL 60532
(312) 968-0074

National Audubon Society,
Clyde E. Buckley Wildlife Sanctuary
Rural Route #3
Frankfort, KY 40601
(606) 873-5711

National Parks & Conservation
Association
1701 18th Street N.W.
Washington, D.C. 20009
(202) 265-2717

The Nature Center of Charlestown
P.O. Box 82
Devault, PA 19432
(215) 935-9777

North Carolina Marine Resources
Center at Roanoke Island
P.O. Box 967
Manteo, NC 27954
(919) 473-3493

Sagamore Conference Center
Sagamore Road
Raquette Lake, NY 13436
(518) 354-5311

Science Center of New Hampshire
P.O. Box 173
Holderness, NH 03245
(603) 968-7194

Tennessee Valley Authority–Land
Between the Lakes
Golden Pond, KY 42231
(502) 924-5602

Touch of Nature
Environmental Center
Southern Illinois University at
Carbondale
Carbondale, IL 62901
(618) 529-4161

George Williams College/Lake
Geneva Campus Program Dept.
Box 210
Williams Bay, WI 53191
(414) 245-5531

Woods Hole Oceanographic
Institution
Woods Hole, MA 02543
(617) 548-1400

Zoological Society of Cincinnati
3400 Vine Street
Cincinnati, OH 45220
(513) 281-3700

Government & Public Administration

American Federation of State,
County, and Municipal Employees
1625 L Street N.W.
Washington, D.C. 20026
(202) 452-4800

Better Government Association
230 North Michigan Avenue,
Suite 1710
Chicago, IL 60601
(312) 641-1181

The Brookings Institution
1775 Massachusetts Avenue N.W.
Washington, D.C. 20036
(202) 797-6210

Congress Watch
213 Pennsylvania Avenue S.E.
Washington, D.C. 20003
(202) 546-4996

Copus
1 Dupont Circle, Suite 500
Washington, D.C. 20036
(202) 659-1747

The Michael Curry Internship
Program, Office of the
Governor of Illinois
202 State House
Springfield, IL 62706
(217) 782-4775

Democratic National Committee
1625 Massachusetts Avenue N.W.
Washington, D.C. 20036
(202) 797-6555

Governor's Intern Program
State of Georgia
Office of the Governor
State Capitol
Atlanta, GA 30334
(404) 656-1794

Governor's Internship Program,
State of Florida
The Capitol
Tallahassee, FL 32301
(904) 488-4505

Independent Sector
1828 L Street N.W.
Washington, D.C. 20036
(202) 223-8100

Maine State Government Summer
Internship Program
Bureau of Public Administration
University of Maine at Orono
Orono, ME 04469
(207) 581-4136

Massachusetts Internships Office
330 Stuart Street
Boston, MA 02116
(617) 727-8688

Metropolitan Washington Council of
Governments
1875 I Street N.W.
Suite 200
Washington, D.C. 20006
(202) 223-6800

National Security Agency,
Department of Defense
Fort Meade, MD 20755-6000
Attn: M322/Summer
(301) 859-4590

National Women's Political Caucus
1275 K Street N.W.
Suite 750
Washington, D.C. 20005
(202) 898-1100

The North Carolina State
Government Internship Program
Youth Advocacy and Involvement
Office
121 West Jones Street
Raleigh, NC 27603
(919) 733-9296

Northeast Midwest Congressional
Coalition
530 House Annex 2
Washington, D.C. 20515
(202) 226-3920

Office of the Governor
State of Idaho Statehouse
Boise, ID 83720
(208) 334-2100

Office of the Governor
State of Iowa Capitol Building
Des Moines, IA 50319
(515) 281-5211

Office of the Governor
State of Michigan
State Capitol Building
Lansing, MI 48909
(517) 373-3430

Office of the Governor
State of Missouri
P.O. Box 720
Jefferson City, MO 65102
(314) 751-3222

Office of the Governor
State of New York
State Capitol
Albany, NY 12224
(518) 474-4623

Office of the Governor
State of Oklahoma
State Capitol Building
Oklahoma City, OK 73105
(405) 521-2342

Office of the Governor, State of Texas
State Capitol Building
Austin, TX 78711
(512) 475-4101

Office of the Governor
State of Vermont
State House
Montpelier, VT 05602
(802) 828-3333

Office of the Governor
State of Wisconsin
P.O. Box 7863
Madison, WI 53707-7863
(608) 266-1212

Office of the Vice President of the
United States
Old Executive Office Building
Washington, D.C. 20500
(202) 456-2326

Republican National Committee
310 1st Street S.E.
Washington, D.C. 20003
(202) 863-8500

State of South Dakota Executive
Intern Program
700 North Illinois
Kneip Building
Pierre, SD 57501
(605) 773-3777

United States Nuclear Regulatory
Commission
Washington, D.C. 20555
(301) 492-8275

United States Senate Committee on
Aging
Dirksen Building, Room G-33
Washington, D.C. 20510
(202) 224-5364

Museums, Cultural & Historical Organizations

Alaska State Museum
Pouch FM
Juneau, Alaska 99811
(907) 465-2901

American Council for the Arts
570 Seventh Avenue
New York, NY 10018
(212) 354-6655

Anacostia Neighborhood Museum
2404 Martin Luther King Jr. Avenue
S.E.
Washington, D.C. 20020
(202) 287-3369

Baltimore Museum of Art
Art Museum Drive
Baltimore, MD 21218
(301) 396-6320

Baltimore Museum of Industry
1415 Key Highway
Baltimore, MD 21230
(301) 727-4808

Brockton Art Museum
Fuller Memorial
Oak Street
Brockton, MA 02401-1399
(617) 588-6000

The Brooklyn Museum
Eastern Parkway
Brooklyn, NY 11238
(718) 638-5000

The Children's Museum
Museum Wharf
300 Congress Street
Boston, MA 02210
(617) 426-6500

The Corcoran Gallery of Art
17th Street and New York Avenue
N.W.
Washington, D.C. 20006
(202) 638-3211

Denver Art Museum
100 West 14th Avenue Parkway
Denver, CO 80204
(303) 575-2793

David Findlay, Jr., Inc.
41 East 57th Street
New York, NY 10022
(212) 486-7660

Freer Gallery of Art
Smithsonian Institution
12th Street and Jefferson Drive S.W.
Washington, D.C. 20560
(202) 357-2253

Hirshhorn Museum and Sculpture
Garden
Smithsonian Institution
Washington, D.C. 20560
(202) 357-3235

Historic Bethlehem, Inc.
501 Main Street
Bethlehem, PA 18108
(215) 868-6311

Hudson River Museum
Trevor Park-on-Hudson
511 Warburton Avenue
Yonkers, NY 10701
(914) 963-4550

Huguenot Historical Society
P.O. Box 339
New Paltz, NY 12561
(914) 255-1660

Huntsville Museum of Art
700 Monroe Street
Huntsville, AL 35801
(205) 534-4566

Informative Design Group, Inc.
2201 Wisconsin Avenue,
Suite 390
Washington, D.C. 20007
(202) 785-3330

Jacksonville Museum of Arts and
Sciences
1025 Gulf Life Drive
Jacksonville, FL 32207
(904) 396-9906

Joslyn Art Museum
2200 Dodge Street
Omaha, NE 68102-1292
(402) 342-3300

Library of Congress
Washington, D.C. 20540
(202) 287-5220

Los Angeles County Museum of Art
5905 Wilshire Boulevard
Los Angeles, CA 90036
(213) 857-6067

The Metropolitan Museum of Art
Office of Academic Affairs
Fifth Avenue at 82nd Street
New York, NY 10028

Minnesota Museum of Art
St. Peter at Kellogg
St. Paul, MN 55102
(612) 292-4355

Museum of Broadcasting
1 East 53rd Street
New York, NY 10022
(212) 752-4690

Museum of Fine Arts
465 Huntington Avenue
Boston, MA 02115
(617) 267-9300

Museum of Fine Arts/George Walter
Vincent Smith Art Museum
49 Chesnut Street
Springfield, MA 01103
(413) 732-6092

National Air and Space Museum
NASM Internship Program
P-700
Washington, D.C. 20560
(202) 357-1504

National Building Museum
Pension Building
Judiciary Square N.W.
Washington, D.C. 20001
(202) 272-2495

National Museum of African Art
316 A Street N.E.
Washington, D.C. 20002
(202) 287-3490

National Museum of American Art
Committee on Professional Programs
8th and G Streets N.W.
Washington, D.C. 20560
(202) 357-2714

National Museum of American
History
Office of Public and Academic
Programs
Room 4609
Smithsonian Institution
Washington, D.C. 20560
(202) 357-1300

National Portrait Gallery
Education Department, Room 195
F Street at 8th N.W.
Washington, D.C. 20560
(202) 357-2920

National Trust for Historic
Preservation
Center for Preservation Training
1785 Massachusetts Avenue N.W.
Washington, D.C. 20036

Appendix 2

Books for Further Reference

Choosing a Career

1. *The Right Move: How to Find the Perfect Job*, Ballantine Books, 1987. Michael Zey, management and career consultant, takes you through the steps to finding the perfect job. He offers information on tangibles such as perks and benefits and intangibles such as politics and pressure. The book doesn't just list companies, it examines their character.

2. *Where Do I Go from Here with My Life?*, Ten Speed Press, 1974. Specifically for those who often have difficulty getting interesting jobs: high school students, housewives, those who hate nine-to-five schedules, restless retirees.

3. *The New York Times Career Planner*, Random House, 1987. General advice on how to choose a career for the recent college graduate. The book examines 101 opportunities in interesting professions.

4. *The Harvard Guide to Careers*, Harvard University Press, 1987. Provides information on scores of fields, including advertising, banking and government.

5. *The Right Job*, Penguin Books, 1987. Robert O. Snelling, Sr., the director of one of the nation's largest employment services, shares his strategy on how to scour the job market for a career that best suits your skills and interests.

6. *The Job Rated Almanac*, Pharos Books, 1988. 250 jobs are ranked by salary, working conditions, stress, travel opportunities, growth potential, physical demands, benefits and job security. The data are from the Bureau of Labor Statistics, the Department of Commerce and the Census Bureau.

7. *The Three Boxes of Life*, Ten Speed Press, 1978. This is essentially a book of ideas about school, work and retirement.

8. *The 100 Best Companies to Work For in America*, New American Library, 1984. America's top companies, from the employee's point of view, are rated on pay, growth potential and work environment. (Did you know that IBM and Dupont have eighteen-hole employee golf courses?)

9. *Wanted: Liberal Arts Graduates*, Doubleday, 1987. For liberal arts graduates looking for work in business and the arts. Includes an index of major companies who employ liberal arts graduates.

10. *Lit. Biz. 101: How to Get Happily, Successfully Published*, Dell, 1988. How to get the best deal when negotiating with agents, editors, periodicals or publishing houses in the areas of fiction, genre writing, ghost writing, children's books, scriptwriting, magazine and newspaper writing.

11. *What Color Is Your Parachute?*, Ten Speed Press, 1989. This whimsical book emphasizes self-assessment as the primary tool in choosing a career. Published annually, the book includes several self-assessment exercises.

12. *Jobs! What They Are . . . Where They Are . . . What They Pay!*, Simon & Schuster, 1989. A comprehensive directory of twenty-nine career fields and scores of specific jobs. Packed with information, it reads like a catalogue.

13. *The School of Visual Arts Guide to Careers*, McGraw-Hill, 1987. Valuable "how to" tips for any student who wants to work in fields ranging from photography and art direction to film, video and the fine arts. Interviews with twenty-six visual arts luminaries like Bob Giraldi and Milton Glaser.

14. *Power Failure*, St. Martin's Press, 1989. Why women said "No" to management positions—six inside stories to help others say "Yes." This personal book gives nitty-gritty insight into business politics and relations.

15. *So You Want to Be in Advertising*, Simon & Schuster, 1988. A career copywriter and creative director at four top agencies gives advice on finding, and keeping, an advertising job. Practical hints on portfolios, layout, photo shoots, editing and teamwork.

16. *168 More Businesses Anyone Can Start and Make a Lot of Money*, Bantam Books, 1984. Descriptions of exciting, take-charge businesses with low capital investments and high yields. Real-life examples include spaghetti outlets, videocassette rental stores, concessions at country fairs, dance machines, wall printing, hospitality services. The book doesn't promise easy money, but rather success through hard work.

17. *Inside Track: How to Get Into and Succeed in America's Prestige Companies*, Vintage Books, 1986. What is it really like to work for the prestige companies? Information on major American companies, including Xerox, Lorimar Telepictures, Mattel, etc., ranging from what's overheard at the water cooler to vital statistics.

18. *Career Development*, Prentice-Hall, 1989. A career consultant gives advice. Emphasis is placed on self-testing to discover your skills and interests.

Experience Abroad/Travel

19. *Abroad and Beyond*, Cambridge University Press, 1988. Two university professors investigate numerous study programs here and abroad. It is a good book to read to help you decide if you want to study abroad. Includes information on costs, contacts and preparation.

20. *The Teenager's Guide to Study, Travel and Adventure Abroad*, St. Martin's Press, 1988. Evaluates over 150 programs abroad. Includes interviews with students who have already gone on the programs and gives insight into their pros and cons.

21. *Taking Off*, Simon & Schuster, 1989. Extraordinary ways to spend your first year out of college, including teaching English in China, living on an Israeli kibbutz, helping the homeless, working in a Central American refugee camp and saving endangered wildlife. It explains how a productive "year off" makes you more interesting and therefore more employable.

22. *Learning Vacations*, Peterson's Guides, 1986. Alternative ways to spend vacations, including joining archaeological digs, safaris, whale-watching excursions, art and cultural tours, writers' conferences. The book is a compilation of lists and, although informative, reads like one.

Succeeding on the Job

23. *How to Make $1,000 a Minute*, Ten Speed Press, 1987. When and how to ask for a raise—more often than not a touchy, perspiration-filled experience.

24. *In Search of Excellence: Lessons from America's Best-Run Companies*, Harper & Row, 1982. Eight practices that lead to successfully managed companies.

25. *How to Work for a Jerk: Your Success Is the Best Revenge*, Vintage Books, 1987. How to deal with your boss.

26. *Glamour Guide to Office Smarts*, Fawcett Columbine, 1986. Helps you track your first year on the job. Covers productivity, office politics, rapport building with your boss and peers and job satisfaction.

27. *What They Don't Teach You at Harvard Business School*, Bantam Books, 1984. This engaging book teaches "street smarts": the ability to make active, positive use of your instinct, insight and perceptions. Learn how to apply "people sense" in business to get things done. Key chapters on reading other people and yourself.

28. *Leader Effectiveness Training*, Bantam Books, 1977. Get people to work with you, not just for you. Helps you to resolve conflicts and raise productivity.

29. *Guerrilla Marketing Attack*, Houghton Mifflin, 1989. New strategies for winning big profits for small businesses. Pleasurable and informative reading.

30. *How to Sell Your Ideas*, McGraw-Hill, 1984. Persuasion as an art. Teaches techniques to make your ideas come alive in other people's minds. The book describes the subtle, yet powerful forces that undermine persuasion and how to deal with them. Learn how to negotiate so all parties are satisfied.

31. *The Vest-Pocket MBA*, Prentice-Hall, 1986. This handbook provides ratios, formulas, guidelines and rules of thumb to help you analyze many business-related problems.

32. *Getting Organized*, Warner Books, 1978. Helps you increase your productivity through financial planning, budgeting your time, organizing your office, rearranging your home.

33. *The Achievement Factors*, Dodd, Mead, 1987. What sets successful people apart from the rest of the pack? Interviews conducted with Nobel laureate Francis Crick, U.S. Supreme Court Justice Sandra Day O'Connor, composer Steve Allen and actor Jack Lemmon show how very different people clear hurdles to success.

Graduate Schools

34. *Essays That Worked for Law Schools*, Mustang Publishing, 1988. Thirty-five essays from successful applications to the nation's top law schools, along with comments from admissions officers

35. *The Official Guide to MBA Programs*, Graduate Management Admissions Council, 1988. Data and information on MBA programs.

Balancing College and Work

36. *Sourcebook for English Papers*, Prentice-Hall, 1987. Can't think of a topic for your psychology term paper? 1001 ideas for term papers, projects, reports and speeches.

37. *Getting Work Experience*, Dell, 1985. Emphasizes the importance of making fieldwork a part of your college experience and outlines the many career-oriented internship programs for college students. The book also offers information on jobs in banking, law, science research, public relations, etc.

38. *10 Steps in Writing the Research Paper*, Barron's Educational Series, 1989. A step-by-step guide to the entire writing process—from topic selection to research to final draft. Recommended for high school, college and graduate work.

39. *Index of Majors*, College Entrance Examination Board, 1988. An index of more than 500 majors at over 3,000 colleges and universities.

40. *Cutting College Costs*, Barnes & Noble, 1988. How to save money in a multitude of ways, including how to get course credit from other colleges, land a work-study job, fund a grant proposal, etc.

41. *Study Tips: How to Study Effectively and Get Better Grades*, Barron's Educational Series, 1983. Schools teach us a lot but never *how* to study. Learn to organize, take notes, read faster and get more out of classroom instruction.

42. *Cultural Literacy: What Every American Needs to Know*, Houghton Mifflin, 1987. An entertaining and informative book, a collection of facts about American culture. It emphasizes the importance of a strong core curriculum.

43. *College: The Undergraduate Experience in America*, Harper & Row, 1987. The results of a three-year study done by the Carnegie Foundation on thirty public and private colleges. It reveals how colleges meet the needs of both the individual and the community and advises potential students to consider both when making college decisions.

Interviews/Résumés

44. *Writing a Job-Winning Résumé*, Prentice-Hall, 1980. Not just another résumé book. Witty chapters like "Making Cents Out of Education" help make résumé writing enjoyable. Step-by-step guidance. When you complete the book (in one evening), you will have completed your résumé.

45. *Sweaty Palms: The Neglected Art of Being Interviewed*, Ten Speed Press, 1984. Richard Nelson Bolles calls this "the best book I know on interviewing." It focuses on how to conduct yourself during an interview and helps you deal

with the butterflies that come with the fear of the unknown. Includes advice on how to dress, present yourself, relax, negotiate salaries, etc.

46. *Polishing Your Professional Image*, American Management Association, 1987. Written by business people for business people. Tips on how to look and act in job interviews and, later, on the job.

47. *Knock 'Em Dead*, Bob Adams, 1987. The best interview comes from preparation. Over 100 great answers to tough interview questions.

Appendix 3

Associations and Organizations for College Students

General Information

No group will satisfy everyone. Before you join an organization, think about who you are, what you'd like to do and how the organization would complement your schoolwork and your long-term goals.

The following list will get you started, but don't stop here. If you're interested in more specialized groups, refer to *The Encyclopedia of Associations* at your local library. Look up opportunities with community groups, local branches of national organizations and voluntary programs in your phone book. Also, check your college catalogue for programs specific to your campus.

Alternative Education

The wide array of alternative education programs available ensures that those seeking a change of pace should be able to find something interesting. If you'd like to try an alternative education program but aren't sure which one to choose, the Association for Experiential Education, C.U. Box 249, Boulder, CO 80309, (303) 492-1547, will help you find the program that fits your interests and abilities.

If you're currently in school, you may be able to get college credit for alternative programs. Check with your registrar before you leave.

Earthwatch
650 Mount Auburn Street, Box 403
Watertown, MA 02272
(617) 926-8200

Offers an array of short expeditions, spanning from coral communities in Fiji to Easter Island cultures.

National Outdoor Leadership School
P.O. Box AA
Lander, WY 82520
(307) 332-6973

Offers a variety of courses, from mountaineering in Alaska to kayaking in Mexico. The program is designed to develop wilderness competence and leadership.

197

The National Theater Institute
Eugene O'Neill Theater Center
305 Great Neck Road
Waterford, CT 06385
(203) 443-7139

According to the institute, 80 percent of its 1,200 alumni are still in the entertainment industry. A semester includes courses in directing, playwriting, costume design, scene design, acting and movement.

Outward Bound USA
384 Field Point Road
Greenwich, CT 06830
(800) 243-8520 or (203) 661-0797

The leader in adventure-based education. Twenty thousand people participated in 1988, so there must be something to their claim that you don't have to be Superman to complete an expedition.

Sea Education Association
P.O. Box 6
Woods Hole, MA 02543
(800) 552-3633 or (508) 540-3954

Semester at Sea
2E Forbes Quadrangle
University of Pittsburgh
Pittsburgh, PA 15260
(800) 854-0195 or (412) 648-7490

Semester at Sea is conducted aboard an ocean liner which stops at exotic ports, while the Sea Education Association's semester is devoted to learning about and sailing on the sea.

Up With People
3103 North Campbell Avenue
Tucson, AZ 85719
(602) 327-7351

Up With People grew from a single theater group in the mid-1960s to five musical theater groups, each one composed of student performers who take ten months to travel to up to eighty cities while living with host families.

Honor Societies and Professional Fraternities

There are hundreds of societies and fraternities that specialize in dozens of areas. Several provide honorary awards and scholarships to their most promising members, and most hold meetings and conferences. Although some groups require that an aspiring member come from a college that has a chapter, some do not. The national organization will be helpful if you'd like to be inducted into a society that's not on your campus, or if you'd like to start a chapter of your own.

Honor Societies

Alpha Lambda Delta
P.O. Box 1576
Muncie, IN 47308
(317) 282-5620

For freshmen with a 3.5 GPA or higher.

Mortar Board
1250 Chambers Road, #170
Columbus, OH 43212-1753
(614) 292-3319

For seniors with a strong academic record and good leadership skills, who have made contributions to their school and community.

Omicron Delta Kappa
Suite 118 Bradley Hall
University of Kentucky
Lexington, KY 40506-0058
(606) 257-5000

Membership in Omicron Delta Kappa, which "recognizes and encourages superior scholarship and leadership," is awarded to juniors and seniors.

Phi Beta Kappa
1811 Q Street N.W.
Washington, D.C. 20009
(202) 265-3808

Phi Kappa Phi
P.O. Box 16000
Louisiana State University
Baton Rouge, LA 70893
(504) 388-4917

Seniors may join Phi Kappa Phi if they are in the top 10 percent of their class; juniors if they are in the top 5 percent.

Professional Fraternities

Business

Beta Gamma Sigma
605 Old Ballas Road, Suite 200
St. Louis, MO 63141
(314) 872-8481

Seniors in the upper 10 percent of their class are eligible for membership, as are juniors in the upper 5 percent.

Engineering

Tau Beta Pi
P.O. Box 8840, University Station
Knoxville, TN 37996-4800
(615) 546-4578

Seniors who are in the top 20 percent of their engineering class and who are well rounded socially and scholastically are considered by Tau Beta Pi.

History

Phi Alpha Theta
2333 Liberty Street
Allentown, PA 18104
(215) 433-4140

For top undergraduates who have completed at least twelve semester hours in history.

Law

Phi Delta Phi
1750 N Street N.W.
Washington, D.C. 20036
(800) 368-5606 or (202) 628-0148

For students who have attended at least one semester of law school and are in good academic standing.

Marketing and Management

Delta Epsilon Chi
1908 Association Drive
Reston, VA 22091
(703) 860-5000

The college division of the high school level Distributive Education Clubs of America, Inc., Delta Epsilon Chi is for students enrolled in marketing and management programs.

Scientific Research

Sigma Xi
345 Whitney Avenue
New Haven, CT 06511
(203) 624-9883

Sigma Xi begins selecting promising research scientists during their junior year.

Job Clearinghouses

The following organizations provide information on internships and jobs with nonprofit organizations around the country.

Community Careers Resource Center
1516 P Street N.W.
Washington, D.C. 20005
(202) 667-0661
The center's main publication, *Community Jobs*, is a monthly tabloid billed as "the only nationwide listing of jobs and internships."

Access
96 Mount Auburn Street
Cambridge, MA 02138
(617) 495-2178
Access produces a large binder, *Opportunities in Community Organizations*; it can be found at over two hundred locations around the country.

Membership Organizations

Many membership societies offer student memberships at reduced cost. Members are usually entitled to free newsletters and information about books, journals, meetings and jobs in the field.

Architecture
The American Institute of Architecture Students
1735 New York Avenue N.W.
Washington, D.C. 20006
(202) 626-7472

Biology

American Institute of Biology
730 11th Street N.W.
Washington, D.C. 20001-1500
(800) 992-AIBS or (202) 628-1500

Broadcasting

Intercollegiate Broadcasting System (IBS)
Box 592
Vails Gate, NY 12584-0592
(914) 565-6710

Although IBS membership is reserved for college radio stations, its yearly National Convention makes it an organization student broadcasters should look into.

Chemistry
The American Chemical Society
1155 16th Street N.W.
Washington, D.C. 20036
(202) 872-4480

Computers

The IEEE Computer Society
1730 Massachusetts Avenue N.W.
Washington, D.C. 20036-1903
(202) 371-0101

Education

National Education Association (NEA)
Student Programs
1201 16th Street N.W., Suite 320
Washington, D.C. 20036
(202) 822-7814

Environmental

Sierra Club
730 Polk Street
San Francisco, CA 94109
(415) 776-2211

In addition to literature and information on meetings, members receive material on group expeditions organized by the club and can participate in its political activities.

Inventions

Inventors Workshop International
3201 Corte Malpaso, Suite 304
Camarillo, CA 93010
(805) 484-9786

Evaluates members' inventions in terms of their manufacturing and marketing potential, and will advise about patents and other protection.

Mathematics

American Mathematical Society
P.O. Box 6248
Providence, RI 02940
(401) 272-9500

The Mathematical Association of America
1529 18th Street N.W.
Washington, D.C. 20036
(202) 387-5200

Music

Music Educators National Conference (MENC)
1902 Association Drive
Reston, VA 22091
(703) 860-4000

Physics

The American Physical Society
335 East 45th Street
New York, NY 10017
(212) 682-7341

Recreation

American Alliance for Health, Physical Education, Recreation and Dance (AHPERD)
1900 Association Drive
Reston, VA 22091
(703) 476-3400

An umbrella organization for several membership organizations, including the American Association for Leisure and Recreation, the Association for the Advancement of Health Education, the National Association for Girls and Women in Sport, the National Association for Sport and Physical Education and the National Dance Association.

Pre-Professional Organizations

Agriculture

FFA
5632 Mount Vernon Memorial Highway
P.O. Box 15160
Alexandria, VA 22309-0160
(703) 360-3600

According to FFA—formerly Future Farmers of America—only 8 percent of the careers in agriculture are in farming. FFA is mainly a high school organization, but interested college students may also join.

Leadership

American Humanics
4601 Madison Avenue, Suite B
Kansas City, MO 64112
(816) 561-6415

Founded to provide leaders for the Boy Scouts, American Humanics is on sixteen campuses, preparing students to work with organizations such as the Red Cross and Boys Clubs of America.

Vocational Training

Vocational Industrial Clubs of
America (VICA)
P.O. Box 3000
Leesburg, VA 22075
(703) 777-8810

VICA operates in vocational high
schools and junior colleges. Its program, a mixture of leadership, citizenship and character development,
is designed to complement vocational skill training.

Social Welfare

If you're a member of a social welfare group on your campus, or if
you'd like to start one, the following organizations can provide you
with resources.

Amnesty International
322 Eighth Avenue
New York, NY 10001
(212) 807-8400

CARE
660 First Avenue
New York, NY 10016-3241
(212) 686-3110

Oxfam America
115 Broadway
Boston, MA 02116
(617) 482-1211

Travel

American Institute for Foreign Study
(AIFS)
102 Greenwich Avenue
Greenwich, CT 06830
(800) 727-AIFS or (203) 869-9090

AIFS offers semester and summer
study programs at fifteen affiliated
colleges and universities worldwide,
including the University of Salzburg
and the University of Paris.

American Youth Hostels (AYH)
P.O. Box 37613
Washington, D.C. 20013-7613
(202) 783-6161

In addition to operating a chain of
inexpensive youth hostels, AYH offers a number of national and international hiking and biking trips,
such as a forty-four-day bike tour
through Europe.

Council on International Educational
Exchange (CIEE)
205 East 42nd Street
New York, NY 10017
(212) 661-1414

Institute of International Education
809 United Nations Plaza
New York, NY 10017-3580
(212) 984-5413

The council and the institute offer,
support or publicize a staggering
number of travel programs of all
sorts, from the Fulbright scholarship
to work in Yugoslavia. Many colleges
are affiliated with these organizations, so getting academic credit for
travel arranged through the council
or the institute should be easy.

International Association of Students
in Economics and Business
Management (AIESEC)
841 Broadway, Suite 608
New York, NY 10003
(212) 979-7400

AIESEC is a French acronym for an
international business exchange program that operates in sixty-seven
countries. If you're interested in
working for a foreign corporation,
AIESEC may have a place for you.

Japan-America Student Conference
606 18th Street N.W., 2nd Floor
Washington, D.C. 20006
(202) 223-4187

The Japan-America Student Conference is held in Japan in odd years and in the United States in even ones. Forty American students join as many Japanese students for a month of study and cultural exchange.

YMCA International Camp
Counselor Program/Abroad
(ICCP/Abroad)
356 West 34th Street, 3rd Floor
New York, NY 10001
(212) 563-3441

Places American camp counselors and workers in foreign camps in over twenty countries. Although students pay an application fee and airfare, the camps provide room and board.

Volunteer Organizations

Groups such as the Red Cross, the Salvation Army, Boy Scouts/Girl Scouts and Big Brothers/Big Sisters are not listed here since these groups act locally. Call your local office for information about activities and opportunities.

General

Campus Outreach Opportunity
League (COOL)
386 McNeal Hall
University of Minnesota
St. Paul, MN 55108
(612) 624-3018

COOL champions student involvement in community service through publications, regional and national meetings and campus organizations. If you want to get involved in your town, COOL can help.

Literacy

The following organizations train volunteers to teach reading using material and instructors provided by the group.

Literacy Volunteers of America
5795 Widewaters Parkway
Syracuse, NY 13214-1846
(315) 445-8000

Laubach Literacy Action
1320 Jamesville Avenue, Box 131
Syracuse, NY 13210
(315) 422-9121

Push Literacy Action Now (PLAN)
1332 G Street S.E.
Washington, D.C. 20003
(202) 547-8903

Reading Is Fundamental (RIF)
600 Maryland Avenue S.W.
Suite 500
Washington, D.C. 20560
(202) 287-3220

Appendix 4

Graduate School: Applying and Getting In

Should You Stay or Should You Go?

It may surprise you that the median age for graduate students in business and law is now twenty-seven. That means that with a graduate degree at twenty-four, you'll be competing with people who have five years of work experience. So, to increase your odds, why not get some work experience after graduation before applying to graduate school? You can earn money, establish your independence and then return to school with a new perspective. (Besides, many companies pay for their employees' graduate work. You could take courses at night and get your degree over four or five years.)

The Exception to the Rule

If you want to become a professor, go directly to graduate school. Do not pass Go, do not collect $200. Academia is competitive on terms of its own which "real world" experience does little to improve.

Applications

If you plan on going straight to graduate school, you'll have to take admissions tests and fill out applications for prospective schools.

Scholarships

You may be eligible for local and national scholarships. Some highly competitive scholarships, like the Rhodes or the Fulbright, require recommendations, interviews, high grades, work experience and athletic achievement. But there are hundreds of other grants available through your school's scholarship office. Check them out.

Entrance Exams

If you've decided to seek another degree beyond your BA, you might have to take one of a battery of tests: GREs, GMATs, LSATs and MCATs, to name a few. Your performance on these tests is one of the factors weighed in the admissions process.

Once you know which field you'd like to do graduate work in, it's a good idea to consult the Graduate School Guide (School Guide Publications, 1-800-433-7771). You can purchase this book or check it out at the library. It contains a list of all the universities in the United States and indicates which degrees each offers. As with your college search years ago, you'll need to make a list, contact the schools, find out their requirements, apply and be interviewed.

A good place to start is with the test itself because your score will help you decide which schools you have a good chance of being admitted to.

Here's a breakdown of the various tests:

GRE: Graduate Record Examination

This test is designed to measure general analytical, quantitative and verbal abilities as well as knowledge and understanding of the subject matter of specific graduate fields. It is required for admission into many graduate and professional schools. There are three parts to the GRE: the General Test, the Subject Test and the Minority Graduate Student Locater Service. The General Test consists of seven thirty-minute sections. There are verbal, mathematical and logical reasoning sections similar to those on the SAT. Scores for this section are reported on a scale of 200 to 800. The fifteen different subject tests (which are administered in biology, chemistry, computer science, economics, education, engineering, geology, history, literature, mathematics, music, physics, political science, psychology and sociology) are intended for students who have majored in each subject in college and are now seeking an advanced degree. They last for two hours and fifty minutes each. Subject test scores are reported on a scale of 200 to 990. The General and Subject tests may be taken on two different dates. Scores are usually reported within four to six weeks. The Minority Graduate Student Locater Service is a free service which does not require taking the GRE; it matches minority students interested in pursuing graduate study with graduate schools seeking minority students. About 20,000 students and 220 schools participate annually.

The GRE is usually given five times a year, in October, December,

February, April, and June. The test is administered at universities throughout the United States and Canada and in many foreign locations. Registration is due about one month before each test date. Fees, as of 1988, are as follows: $35 for the General test and $35 for each Subject test. Computer software and practice tests are available. Further information, practice tests and registration forms can be obtained by writing to GRE, Educational Testing Service, P.O. Box 6000, Princeton, NJ 08541-6000, or by calling ETS at (609) 771-7595.

GMAT: Graduate Management Admissions Test

Required for students applying to business schools, the GMAT contains eight thirty-minute sections. Six are scored while the other two are experimental. The scored sections are as follows: two of regular math (not much harder than the SAT), data sufficiency (regular math concepts posed in more confusing formats), reading passages (three in order of difficulty), grammar (basic concepts tested in "what is wrong with this sentence" format) and analysis of situations (logical reasoning). Scores are usually mailed out about five weeks after the test date.

The GMAT is administered four times a year, in January, March, June and October; registration is due about a month before the test. Test centers are located throughout the United States and Canada and in many foreign locations. The test fee, including five score reports, is $30. For further information, practice tests and registration forms, contact ETS at the above address and phone number.

LSAT: Law School Admissions Test

The LSAT consists of four thirty-five-minute scored sections, as well as a thirty-minute writing sample and two unscored experimental sections. The four scored sections consist of facts and rules (contains outcome and factual questions), arguments (making distinctions between conclusions and assumptions), reading passages (very difficult—simply read for the main idea and refer back for specific questions) and games (involves diagramming problems), followed by the writing sample (this is sent to law schools but it's rumored that they don't use it in making decisions). One distinguishing feature of the LSAT is that no points are subtracted for errors, so lucky guesses can raise your score. Scores are reported within four to six weeks and are on a scale of 10 to 48.

The LSAT is given four times a year, in February, June, September, or October and December; be advised that most law schools require that the LSAT be taken by December to qualify for admission the following fall. Again, there are test centers throughout the United States and in some foreign countries. The fee for the test is $55. For more information, call (215) 968-1001; for an application, call (215) 968-1188.

MCAT: Medical College Admissions Test

The MCAT is designed to test a student's knowledge and understanding of the biology, chemistry and physics designated as prerequisite to the study of medicine. This material is usually that covered in first-year college science courses. The test also evaluates basic analytical ability in solving medically relevant problems. The daylong—8:30 to 6:00—MCAT is divided into four sections: science knowledge (separate biology, chemistry and physics sections), science problems (the three disciplines combined in problems), skills analysis—reading (passages followed by comprehensive questions) and skills analysis—quantitative (questions involving quantitative material). A recent addition to the test is an expository essay section. Scores are given for each of the six sections, on a scale of 1 to 15; they are reported within 45 days.

Given in April and September, the MCAT registration is usually due about a month before the test. The cost is $85. For registration information, write to MCAT registration, ACT, P.O. Box 414, 2555 North Dubuque Road, Iowa City, Iowa, 52243; or call (319) 337-1276.

In addition to the MCAT, there are other medical tests, designed to measure general academic ability as well as science knowledge. These include:

AHPT: Allied Health Professions Test

Required for admission into allied health schools—those that offer programs in such fields as chiropracty, dental technology, midwivery, social work, physical therapy and many other medical professions. Write to AHPT, The Psychological Corporation, 555 Academic Court, San Antonio, TX 78204; or call (512) 270-0396 or (512) 299-1061.

OAT: Optometry Admissions Test

Required for those seeking admission into schools and colleges of optometry. For further information, write to Optometry Admissions Testing Program, 211 East Chicago Avenue, Chicago, IL 60611.

PCAT: Pharmacy College Admissions Test

Required for admission to colleges of pharmacy.

VCAT: Veterinary College Admissions Test

For those seeking admission into colleges of veterinary medicine.

For both of the above, write to The Psychological Corporation at 555 Academic Court, San Antonio, TX 78204, or call (512) 270-0396 or (512) 299-1061.

NTE: National Teachers' Exam

The NTE tests are standardized exams which measure the academic achievements of students who wish to join, or are already admitted to, teacher education programs. There are three types of exams: Core Battery Tests, the nationwide Specialty Area Tests and the statewide Specialty Area Tests. The first of three two-hour-long Core Battery tests is the Test of Communications Skills, which examines listening, reading and writing skills. The second, the Test of General Knowledge, tests understanding of literature and fine arts, mathematics, science and social studies. Finally, the Test of Professional Knowledge assesses the student's aptitude for the types of decisions required of beginning teachers. The scores for this section, however, are not added into the final score. These tests are given in the following subjects: art education, audiology, biology and general science, business education, chemistry and physics, early childhood education, education in the elementary school, education of the mentally retarded, educational administration, English language and literature, French, German, home economics, industrial arts, introduction to the teaching of reading, library media specialist, mathematics, music education, physical education, school guidance and counseling, social studies, Spanish, special education, speech communication and speech-language pathology. There are also state-sponsored Specialty Area Tests in other subjects not covered in the nationwide tests. A single score is reported for each test; for the Core Battery Test there are three scores, on a scale of 600 to 695. Specialty Area scores are reported on a scale of 250 to 999. Scores are usually mailed out within four to six weeks.

Core Battery Tests are usually administered in October, March and June, while Specialty Area Tests are given in November, March and July. Registration closes about one month before each test date. The Core Battery and Specialty Area Tests are taken on different days; you may take one, two or three of the Core tests on the same day and up to two Specialty Area Tests during a special double session given once a year. The cost to take one Core test is $30, two are $50 and three cost $70, while each Specialty test costs $45. For further information, write

NTE Programs, Educational Testing Service, CN 6050, Princeton, NJ 08541-6050, or call (609) 771-7395.

Test Preparation Services

Whether you like them or not, standardized tests are an important part of the graduate school admissions game. They provide an efficient way for admissions officers to discriminate among hundreds of faceless applicants. Fortunately, studying for these tests can improve your scores tremendously.

Many organizations, on and off campus, offer courses which include subject reviews and practice tests as well as strategies to help students "beat" each test. Some test takers swear by these methods while others hesitate to invest so much money in preparing for the exams. (The classes can run upwards of $500.) Below is a description of two of the most popular courses offered nationwide.

Stanley Kaplan

The Kaplan course is for the student who thrives on self-paced study. Students are given review materials to study at home on their own time. They also have the use of the Kaplan Study Center. The center is filled with people taking practice tests, listening to audiotapes and questioning tutors. You can come and go as you please.

Princeton Review

How is the Princeton Review different? First of all the course caters to the student who desires a structured classroom setting. Pupils who display similar weaknesses are grouped together. During weekly lectures, techniques and concepts are taught. Workshops may be attended for further practice. Private tutoring is also available.

What Else Determines Admission?

Test scores, college grade point average, activities, work experience, recommendations and essays are all factors in the selection process.

Let's be realistic. No applicant is strong in all areas. As you complete your application packet, emphasize your strengths and minimize your weaknesses (don't deny them). Begin your applications early and make sure that you give recommenders plenty of time (at least one month). Remember, things always take longer than planned . . . especially things of quality.

Appendix 5

Continuing Your Education Once You Graduate

Graduated does not mean educated.
HARRY EDWARDS, *The Struggle That Must Be*

The real university is a state of mind.
ROBERT M. PIRSIG, *Zen and the Art of Motorcycle Maintenance*

If a well-rounded college education is a combination of academic work and real-world experience, then the best education outside of college comes both on the job and off.

Chances are that once you graduate, you will, at one time or another, be transferred to another city. Keeping yourself busy and meeting new people will become a primary concern. The following suggestions should help.

Continue Taking Classes

"Now that I'm out of school officially, I can concentrate better on the details when I take classes at night," says Scott Freuner, who tries to take courses as much as he can. "I'm in retail and I don't get to stretch my mind academically at work. So in the evenings I take subjects like creative writing or Western civilization. It's fun, it keeps me alert, and because I'm motivated to learn, I'm remembering more than I did in college."

Many people continue their education formally by enrolling in one class every semester. Some may even earn their master's degree through evening courses over a period of years. Others may take classes which don't apply to a degree. A class on Chaucer or immigrants in urban America will help you to remember that there is a world outside your nine-to-five job. It will challenge your mind in ways which are different from your challenges on the job. The contrast is key.

Try taking courses outside a college or university, such as ballroom or salsa dancing, Chinese cooking or pottery making. Seminars are typically sponsored in every city. You may want to take a Saturday course in public speaking or how to use software. Even if your company will not pay, you may want to participate.

Attend Museum and Library Lectures

"Once a month on Tuesday nights, a friend and I go to a yearlong series of lectures at our local library," says Hank Sands, an architect. "Last month the lecture was by a professor on the tropical rain forests, about which I knew little before I attended. After the talk, I went and checked out a book the lecturer recommended. I may never be an expert on any of these subjects, but over time I'll know a little about a lot of things."

Most museums and libraries offer free or affordable lecture series on topics ranging from extraterrestrials to creative writing to the life cycle of vampire bats. The lectures are given by professionals in the field. Usually the people in the audience are interesting too.

Register for Weekend Seminars

"My weekend seminar on management training was more like a mini-vacation," says Adele Hayward, who manages an office of temporary personnel. "We broke into several different groups and discussed key issues in management: how to hire the best people, how to keep them motivated, how to give people constructive criticism. I met many interesting people, including someone who made me a job offer two weeks later."

There are seminars every weekend on topics ranging from wine tasting to finance and accounting. Some of the seminars are in retreat areas in the mountains and are both educational and recreational.

Join or Form a Book or Writing Club

In every city there are informal groups where books or writing are discussed. This is a great way to make friends. You may want to form your own reading/dinner clubs to discuss classics you never read or current literature.

"My book club is like an extended family," says Margaret Maillor, a freelance photographer, who formed a club with her friends three years ago. "We've read everything from *Origin of Species* to *The Bonfire of the*

Vanities. It's been fascinating to learn different things about your friends through their interpretations of each book. We all refrain from being judgmental. Sometimes that's hard. We get into some pretty rigorous debates at times.''

Outdoor Clubs

These clubs offer a variety of activities, such as hiking, canoeing, camping, sailing and skiing. Sometimes weekend group trips are available to your favorite mountain or resort.

Pat Sullivan's membership in the Audubon Society led her to a career. Because of her affection for waterfowl Pat often joined the Society for excursions to rookeries along the Atlantic coast. On one of these trips she met a researcher from a prestigious Midwestern zoo. After they spent the weekend together she offered Pat a job. Six months later Pat was in Cincinnati conducting ornithological research.

Computer Groups

If you have a computer with the proper modem, you can hook it up to your telephone and exchange information and play games with other computer buffs across the country. You may also want to try your hand at co-authoring a software program.

Free Concerts

Most cities feature free concerts or plays in the summer. You can pack a picnic and a blanket and relax listening to Verdi's *Aïda* while gazing up at the stars. If your city doesn't have a series of park concerts, check the churches and synagogues. They often feature classical music concerts.

"Summer wouldn't be summer without concerts at Wolftrap," says Richard Harrin, a congressional aide in Washington. "Music under the stars, a picnic on the grass and wine with your friends is one the best ways to spend a Saturday night. It's a close second to a night at the ball game.''